Prophesying upon the Bones

J. Reuben Clark

PROPHESYING UPON THE BONES

J. Reuben Clark and the
Foreign Debt Crisis,
1933-39

GENE A. SESSIONS

UNIVERSITY OF ILLINOIS PRESS
Urbana and Chicago

Frontispiece courtesy of the LDS Church Historical
Department Archives. Used by permission.

This book is printed on acid-free paper.

Library of Congress Cataloging-in-Publication Data
Sessions, Gene Allred.
    Prophesying upon the bones : J. Reuben Clark and the foreign dept
crisis, 1933-39 / Gene A. Sessions.
        p.   cm.
    Includes index.
    ISBN 0-252-01927-X
    1. Investments, American—History. 2. Bonds—United States—
History. 3. Debts, External—History. 4. Foreign Bondholders
Protective Council, inc. —History. 5. Clark, J. Reuben (Joshua
Reuben), 1871-1961. 6. Mormons—United States—Biography.
I. Title.
HG4538.S44 1992
332.6' 7373'09043—dc20   91-45054
                                                                CIP

For Jerry

Give short shift to all these slant-eyed schemes of designing revolutionists against the existing order, which has been born and bred of the wisdom of the ages and of the sacrifice and blood of your ancestors.

—J. Reuben Clark

Contents

Preface

By the end of the 1980s, the international debt situation had degenerated into such a colossal mess, particularly in the so-called Third World, that even the most solemn observers were throwing their hands in the air. Henry Kissinger bluntly informed creditor nations that "none of the major debtor nations will be able simultaneously to pay its debt, achieve economic growth and maintain its political and social equilibrium." A group of clerics calling itself the Interfaith Action for Economic Justice advocated for a wholesale cancellation of the Third World debt, labeling it immoral and illegitimate, having "already been paid because the natural resources, raw material and human labor have been expropriated by the colonial powers for over 100 years." The Bush administration urged banks to forgive voluntarily part of the $410 billion owed them from Third World governments as an alternative to the formation of an international agency that could require writing off some of the loans. Some pundits predicted that a mass failure of foreign debt service would precipitate a major crisis in the U.S. banking system that would make the savings-and-loan disaster look like the good old days.

Reacting to such gloomy realizations, financial experts in the industrial world began a frantic scramble to find some answers short of surrender that might salvage at least something out of the situation, but an abundance of dilemmas confounded the most savvy economists and politicians. Some very sober voices in the whole cacophony called for a "politicization" of the problem, perhaps through the creation of international understandings that would reflect, according to Kissinger, "a realistic schedule for debt payments and above all a reciprocal commitment to renewed growth and development." Such a framework would encourage banks "to give up the pretense that full debt service is possible and forego the contortions required to keep the myth alive."

In the midst of all the technical jargon and diplomatic pontification over the issue, it became easy to miss the real significance of that great myth. Not so long ago, in a world since gone away, the sacred obligation to repay debts, no matter what the exigencies, comprised one of the great pillars upon which the very universe rested in equilibrium. In the 1980s, however, few contemporary analysts worried about such philosophical fluff or remembered that a half-century before, a valiant knight from that crumbling world had tried desperately to shore up international fiscal responsibility as his part of a last-ditch effort at saving the old universe. As the Great Depression smashed into gravel the rock of governmental credit, millions of dollars in foreign securities had gone into default, many of them in the hands of private American bondholders. Believing that an acquiescence to such failures signaled an unacceptable abandonment of a major underpinning of civilization, a conservative international lawyer named J. Reuben Clark, Jr., who believed himself to be a literal prophet of God, took command of a federally sanctioned organization called the Foreign Bondholders Protective Council and led a heroic effort to reinvigorate the failing debts through the very darkest days of the 1930s. Surprisingly, he won some major victories in the war and retired to his home in Utah convinced that in the very least the world had learned a serious lesson from its ill-conceived foreign lending habits. Perhaps ensuing events have proven him dead wrong, but other prophets from Jeremiah to John the Baptist to Cotton Mather had struggled unsuccessfully against the trends of the times only to proclaim to the end the immutability of truth.

With that perspective in mind, there follows hereafter a study of an imposing personality and an equally imposing problem. Inasmuch as conflict is an essential ingredient to a good story, this ought to be a whale of a fine tale, but in it is also plenty of meaning. We might call it something of a parable in the biblical sense, an allegorical epic filled with the struggle between God's ordered truth and the chaotic tendencies of a wicked world. The major character and his crusade could not fit the prescription any better were they the products of imagination.

Growing up after World War II in the midst of the Rocky Mountains, I became quickly aware of the omnipresence of J. Reuben Clark in our provincial world. A high leader in the Mormon church, he would come on television during the conferences of the church and appear often in pictures in the *Deseret News*. It seemed to me that he was so very old; he had a chubby face, thick lips that were always smiling, and a venerable shock of white hair. In the back of everyone's mind in Mormondom was the notion that "President Clark" had done something in the government, that he was famous outside of Utah. But something else about him set him apart. He *always* talked about old and solid values and a system of social beliefs based upon a legendary time not so long ago when everybody tried to do what was right, worked hard, raised big families, and feared the Lord. If ever there was an image of something old, it was Reuben Clark. When he died at the age of ninety in 1961, his impact upon me and the rest of the Mormons in our accelerating world was undeniable. We could not go quite so fast, and perhaps we even felt the need to turn around.

When I left the mountain fastnesses of my youth, I discovered that Reuben Clark was not so famous. The only mention of him in history books had to do with something called "the Clark Memorandum." I also found, however, that he did spend his prime years in public service, and that for more than three decades he spoke in the national forum for his system of beliefs during a time when America was transforming itself in what Frederick Lewis called "the Big Change." For Clark there could be no change because truth was truth, and the God-ordained order of things was as inviolable as holy writ.

In 1933, Clark had reached the apparent end of his national service, having accepted a position in the ruling triumvirate of the Mormon priesthood. But a mammoth threat to his structured world had emerged in the ugly form of the Great Depression. So he picked up the cudgel and plunged once again into battle to defend the bastions of the old universe by preserving international fiscal responsibility. This story is about that fight, about one molluscan, hard-thinking person who refused to accept the fallibility of the mythological constructs of the incredible history of invincible America. As Peter Morton has put it, Clark came to personify "the old order dying hard, contesting every inch of the terrain."

Nearly one-third of some $6 billion worth of foreign bonds afloat in the United States were in some stage of default when Franklin D. Roosevelt, the harbinger of the new era, gave his first inaugural address in 1933. Some debtors had come to believe that their obligations, in the face of world economic dysfunction, were void, and that the creditor nations and their citizens were simply the unfortunate victims of something over which no one had any control. In response to this crisis and following the lead of other creditor governments, the Roosevelt administration initiated the creation of the Foreign Bondholders Protective Council (FBPC) to work toward a revitalization of the foreign dollar bonds. J. Reuben Clark became the first functioning president of this group and proved, as one State Department functionary remembered, to be extremely stubborn and acquisitive in his efforts.

For almost five years, Reuben Clark *was* the council, imbuing it with all of his ideals concerning international morality, nationalist isolationism, and the certain sanctity of the American cause and of the old order— hard work, thrift, self-sufficiency, and strict economic responsibility on a personal as well as international level. He fought off a concerted attack that opponents waged against the council and used his many years of skill as a diplomat to win the favor of an anti-big business administration in Washington and to make remarkable progress in bringing life into a good portion of the sagging dollar bonds. All of this time, Clark waged a vigorous war upon the new order on another front. In his ecclesiastical position, and between terms in the council office in New York, he strove desperately with his Mormons to bring about a new communitarianism that would remove them from the horrors of the New Deal and its welfare statism.

The reader may surmise from the above that this work began as social and intellectual history and drifted inevitably into ecomomic history, although it certainly would not qualify for what Charles Kindleberger has termed historical economics, in which economists analyze processes and structures. It does not, for example, attempt a detailed reporting of the negotiations the FBPC carried forth with the various debtor governments, referring the reader instead to the council's published annual reports. Nevertheless, it may help to redress the grievance contained in Peter Lindert's rephrasing of George Santayana: "The international financial community has often preferred to repeat the past rather than study it." I hope to chronicle generally a portion of international debt negotiations during the 1930s and to provide an analytical coverage of the complicated problems the defaulted foreign bond situation created. I have also attempted a deep probe into the mindset of a representative nineteenth-century American who refused to believe that the old universe of fiscal responsibility was suddenly dead without hope of revival. This book deals largely with the actions and thoughts of one person, but it is not in a pure sense biography. Against the backdrop of the plight of people who held foreign bonds, the drama is portrayed of an unyielding prophet attempting to resurrect the bones of a former world. This work ought to appeal not only to those wishing to understand the history of the foreign bond situation in the 1930s but also to students of American intellectual history, interested in contemplating the ways in which the Great Depression and its related dysfunctions forced a painful readjustment of the ways in which Americans defined economic and social reality. The struggles of such conservatives as J. Reuben Clark to stave off this change provide a fascinating perspective from which to survey the entire period.

I do not wish to append here a prolix compendium of all of the people who have contributed to this work over the past two decades it has been in production, if for no other reason than that I cannot possibly remember them all. There are a few, however, whose acts of assistance demand recognition. William Miller and Thomas Campbell at Florida State University provided the intellectual and diplomatic history perspectives that combined to create the idea for this book. Personal support and advice came abundantly from Christine Brand, Lola Sessions, and Stephen Stathis. Among those who helped with various stages of preparing the manuscript were Laura Duncan, Suzanne Chapple, Dorothy Draney, Marilee Sackolwitz, Cindy Hooper, and Myrna Eberle. Kristi Chase performed the final task of putting the whole thing into a word processor and deserves particular credit for patience and long-suffering. Sterling Sessions of the College of Business and Economics at Weber State University read the manuscript to see that it had not slipped any cogs in that direction. My friend and colleague in the Department of Economics at Weber State, Richard Alston, checked me on the basics of international economics and allowed me access to his research materials for a chapter on the subject in his forthcoming economics textbook. The greatest support of all came from my partner Shantal Hiatt and my late colleague and dear friend Jerome Bernstein. They kept spice in my life while I labored on the project.

John R. Petty and Alice M. Popp, respectively president and secretary of the Foreign Bondholders Protective Council in the mid-1980s when I finished the body of research on the project, went out their way to provide assistance, as did Dennis Rowley at the Harold B. Lee Library at Brigham Young University where the Clark papers reside. Institutional cooperation and support came freely from Florida State University, the National Archives, the Library of Congress, the Historical Department of the LDS Church, and Weber State University. I am particularly grateful to WSU

Presidents Rodney Brady, Stephen Nadauld, and Paul Thompson, and Academic Vice President Robert Smith, who generously provided time and financial support toward the completion of this endeavor. And for the second time in my career, I offer my deepest thanks to Richard Wentworth, Elizabeth Dulany, and the others at the University of Illinois Press. For whatever is wrong with this work, I stand all alone.

Prophesying upon the Bones

CHAPTER

1

The End of the Nineteenth Century

The hand of the Lord was upon me,
and carried me out in the spirit of the Lord,
and set me down in the midst of the valley which was
full of bones, . . .

In their jittery but characteristic optimism, Americans have always celebrated a kind of High Mass to wild hope at the coming of a new year. It seems that the more difficult and ill the past year, the more Americans look to the new one for goodness and health. They believe with a strange mysticism that somehow the passing of time by some artificially designated point converts old and disparaging problems into new ones with easier solutions. They participate in rituals of drunkenness or prayer, ribaldry or worship, all in the belief that things must get better. There always appears a new scheme or new leader on the horizon. The promised land lies always over the next hill and beyond the next miracle.

The coming of 1933 brought perhaps the epitome of such an American rite of hope. Indeed, the nineteenth century in America, at least with regard to economic truisms, had come to a crashing finish in 1929 with the onslaught of the Great Depression. Then had come what Gilbert Seldes solemnly called the "years of the locust," 1929 to 1932, years of mordant failure, dreadful portent, and blackening despair.[1] Herbert Hoover, holding true to the gospel of laissez-faire, continued to believe that the current dysfunction would reverse itself automatically with as little prodding from the government as possible. Despite his assurance that his modest program would succeed, the president's formalistic philosophy actually made the depression go from bad to worse (witness his endorsement of the Smoot-Hawley Tariff of 1930). By the end of 1932, however, cold and ugly facts made it increasingly difficult for people to swallow Hoover's seemingly naive optimism. National income had fallen to half that of 1929 while unemployment had risen between fourteen and fifteen million. Hoover retained his composure, however. His head perched atop his starched collar, he projected the veritable image of late-nineteenth-century America and of the old universe—Newtonian, balanced, and perfect. Always the "great engineer," he symbolized an ever-increasing abundance emanating from inexhaustible and indomitable American ingenuity and managerial prowess. The notion of chaos could find no place in his dogma.

By December 31, 1932, even the defeated president, preparing to escape the White House like a scapegoat on the Day of Atonement, realized that something had gone terribly wrong with the old order of things. The carefully tooled gears no longer meshed, and the entire social and economic cosmos seemed to be crumbling. As Americans looked back upon the old year, the election of Franklin Roosevelt seemed the only hopeful augury—and some were not so sure about that. Nothing felt right any more. The best hopes of the ebullient twenties were dying in the morass of some mysterious ailment in the democratic-capitalist system. World peace dreams, epitomized in the ingenuous Kellogg Peace Pact of 1928, faded rapidly as nations failed to agree on disarmament and as the Japanese threatened to upset the status quo in East Asia and the Pacific. At home, neither unemployment, nonproduction, nor panic would yield to old-fashioned remedies. Maybe the end of democracy and capitalism had come. Perhaps Marx prophesied truly after all. But for Americans, there was always another year, another hope, another dream, another leader—another miracle.

There could be little doubt that the New Year's celebration would be one to remember. The editors of the nation's newspapers sensed it. Something about contemplating 1933 excited even the calmest observers. "Americans look to 1933 with chastened optimism," wrote one editor, "but nevertheless with relief and hope. . . . Good riddance to 1932."[2] After noting "the sort of paradox with which Americans are starting upon 1933," another one sensed a "better feeling" in the land. "But if you press an economist or banker or industrialist or merchant or ordinary man in the street to give a precise reason for the faith that is in him, he will confess himself unable to do it."[3]

In retrospect, it is not difficult to see good, or at least some, reason for this optimism. After so long in the doldrums of stale ideas, at last the promise of some alternate—if somewhat nebulous—answers had arrived. Those in the forefront, of course, emanated from Hyde Park and the president-elect, but there were others. "Technocracy," for example, typified the fashionable trend toward national planning in the early thirties. Its leader and noisy spokesperson, an engineer named Howard Scott, expanded upon the writings of Thorstein Veblen in a cryptic call for a machinelike "system of centrally allocated resources and efficiently administered production."[4] By New Year's Eve 1932, Technocracy had become if nothing else a popular subject of conversation at parties. The Technocrats, went the joke, had decided what to do with everything but lame ducks.[5] The more intellectual and radical "collectivists" in the national planning movement believed that they had seen the vision of their new system replace capitalism as capitalism had replaced feudalism. Based essentially on pragmatism, American collectivism attracted many thinkers and then filtered through the media to the masses. Such leading collectivists as Howard Lee McBain, dean of Columbia University Graduate Faculties, told Americans that they must forget their outmoded ideas of individualism and nationalism and submit themselves to increasing guidance, compulsion, restraint, and control: "We have no alternative."[6] So, in addition to other less tangible forces, fresh ideologies wafted through the land. Like a drowning swimmer in search of air, the person on the street would breathe anything.

This feeling of a coming new age permeated America that Saturday night, December 31, 1932, a time for forgetting troubles and for raising high the strains of hope. In New York, much liquor flowed at low prices. The police cooperated by looking the other way and conducting no raids that night. Many glasses rose in toasts to the coming end of Prohibition, and the crowds in the hotels and on the streets sang "Happy Days Are Here Again."[7] Such classic revelry belied the sorry state of the Union. The nonsensical became important as people tried to forget and to believe. For example, Thelma Atterbury from Terre Haute, who danced under the name of Feon Vanmar in the Ziegfeld Follies, made front-page headlines that night when she became so happily inebriated at a Long Island party that she fell off a porch and broke her jaw.[8]

The earth revolved on its axis a final time under the onerous name of 1932, and morning dawned on a beautiful 1933 Sunday on the East Coast. New York Mayor John P. O'Brien, inaugurated the previous day to replace the scandal-ridden Jimmy Walker, strolled to church in the crisp sunshine of a crystal morning. He told reporters that the glorious weather seemed "auspicious for a return to prosperity."[9] Many of the sermons preached in New York's churches that day echoed O'Brien's prognosis. At the Fifth Avenue Presbyterian Church, the Reverend Dr. Minot C. Morgan declared, "There are indications that the tide that has ebbed so long has begun to turn."[10] In spite of the realities of the depression, the minister's congregation probably already felt warmed inside, for the morning's papers had been full of more than their normal allotment of positive predictions, even for prosperous times. Science was on the march, after all, and would surely solve the world's problems, if only by entertaining the human race into oblivion. Something called television would soon be widespread, New Yorkers read, thanks to developments of 1932. Better radio equipment had also evolved, with improved microphones, transmitters, and receivers.[11] And the British scientist Sir Arthur Stanley Eddington was predicting the imminent smashing of the atom that once harnessed would change the world's entire mode of living.[12] A headline on the front page of the *Times* proclaimed, "Nation Advancing in Fighting Slump," and in the comics, the Winkle family baby wore a bright 1933 banner and carried a suitcase inscribed "better times."[13]

Uptown, at a meeting of the Association for the Advancement of Science, Walter Rautenstrauch, professor of industrial engineering at Columbia and another leading Technocrat, called upon American society to place itself in the hands of the mechanics for a speedy repair job. Appealing to the nation's faith in technical tinkering, and citing its anguish over the dissolution of its old mythological structures, he asked Americans to place their confidence in "those processes of thought and methods of analysis which have enabled the engineer to predict the performance of the machine, the factory, the power plant—even before it is created."[14] Thus, as in a vision from Henry Adams, the Technocrats contributed to a belief on that bright New Year's Day that better times were indeed coming, inasmuch as humankind had it within its genius to solve the depression's socioeconomic riddle. All they asked was that Americans subject themselves to the dynamo; the lost gods would be fair exchange for a new precision universe. "The enterprise of technocracy," they said with characteristic exactitude, "is primarily concerned with the problem of organizing a civilization to maintain itself on a given continental area."[15]

There had never been a more opportune time in the United States for such a worship of the machine as Technocracy suggested. An age for change, for radicalism, the depression era demanded either surrender to chaos or a renewed faith in the human capacity to perceive and create order. As the Reverend Dr. Cleland B. McAfee told his Park Avenue Presbyterian congregation that morning, "We are faced with a pending national revolution unless we develop an internal harmony which involves changes in many of our practices."[16] In a report released to the press that day, the President's Research Committee on Social Trends also emphasized the need for a new sense of community. Warning that unless "there is a speeding up of social invention or a slowing down of mechanical invention, grave maladjustments are certain to result," the six professors on the three-year-old panel laid the blame for America's woes upon the fact that many of the old family-oriented functions of society were slipping from their moorings. Now, without the social stability that the family community had provided in the past, the factory, the school, and the government prevented normal socioeconomic adjustment until even "in the best of years millions of American families are limited to a meagre living."[17]

With 1933, most Americans were ready for that "speeding up of social invention," or at least a new direction, as their choice of Roosevelt had proven. Hoover, no doubt still convinced that grass would grow in the streets as a result of that election, was spending the holidays in Florida. Fishing out of the Palm Beach Sailfish Club on the *Sequoia*, he landed a near- record fish while reportedly considering "various problems, including war debts," but he was talking very little.[18] Indeed, the president had not been on land for a week. The highest administration figure to issue a New Year's statement was Secretary of State Henry Stimson. "The people of our country are suffering continued privations," he said, "but their patience and their courage are unbroken. The new year will offer in this country opportunities for action which are fresh and untried and I put my trust in the resourcefulness and devotion of our people and their chosen leaders."[19] At least Stimson had swallowed the bitter pill.

The politicians being absent, women were the center of the great excitement in Washington that weekend. Mrs. Percy V. Pennybacker and Mrs. Carrie Chapman Catt announced plans for their Eighth Conference on the Cause and Cure of War, to be held in the capital January 17, with six hundred female delegates in attendance representing five million American women. And veteran muckraker Ida M. Tarbell was saying that the "present economic upheaval will make for a better race of people and will find it's solution when parasites are driven from our midst and everybody works."[20] As Tarbell's statement suggested, the thirties were becoming the years of peak interest in the ideas of William Graham Sumner, and it was naturally so because the generation of the thirties had been in school when the thoughts of Sumner, Herbert Spencer, and other Social Darwinists clogged the intellectual arteries of many academicians and pedagogs.[21] But an uglier kind of social theory was also gaining ground by 1933. Washington women were incensed that morning, for example, to read that an Italian physician named Umberto Gabbi was urging his countrywomen to stay away from athletics with Anglo-Saxon females who "are often thick of neck and have herculean arteries, peninsular hands and terrible feet. Family life attracts them but lightly and they are not greatly concerned with modesty."[22]

It was not a large step from applying blanket characteristics to a "race" to blaming the ills of a nation upon a particular ethnic group. The thirties would see history's greatest scourge of racial scapegoating, and Americans were not immune to the dangerous impulse. A Methodist preacher that Sunday morning told his congregation at St. Paul's in New York that the key to understanding the current difficulties lay in discovering the causes of the past ones. He therefore disputed what he called "the obstinate idea deeply rooted in the Jewish mind that earthly prosperity and [well-being] are the normal consequences of rightousness, and conversely, all suffering that of sin."[23] Perhaps one of the most sorrowful results of hard times comes with the vitriol the afflicted tend to heap upon the innocent in an attempt to personify the evils around them into manageable entities. Americans in 1933, believing in the possibility of a solution to their woes, were all too anxious to find someone to blame; for many, such as that Methodist minister, the Jews were eminently handy.

That New Year's Day was a strange sight indeed. After more than three years of economic disaster, it also seemed that the old American good humor was returning as if from an extended journey. Terino, Washington, went on the "wood standard," minting $6,500 worth of wooden coins.[24] Even retreating entrepreneurial capitalism appeared ready to take advantage of the mood for change. No sooner had Senator Dill's committee begun considering the legalization of 3.2 beer[25] than brewing interests began a campaign to show that beer would spur the economy by greatly helping farmers.[26] Nor was old-fashioned American democracy in a terminal condition. In Milwaukee, a street cleaner named John O'Malley had been elected to the Wisconsin legislature on the promise that he would stay out of the clutches of the lobbyists "if I have to live on three donuts a day."[27] And in Indianapolis, the American predilection for prestigious symbols showed itself to be returning to health as aspiring snobs scrambled for low-numbered auto tags—the code: under 20, "bigshot," and under 100, "of considerable influence."[28]

Beneath all of this blithe sense and nonsense lay hard realities nevertheless. Responsible thinkers knew that the current dysfunction would require major corrective measures, and they realized the complexity of the difficulties. Among primary concerns was the international economic situation; slumping trade, problems of foreign exchange, a worsening monetary crisis, and other such headaches preoccupied such officials as Dr. Herbert Feis, the State Department's economic advisor.[29] Problems of transition to a new administration only compounded such knotty difficulties. But for ordinary people, this whole international economic business seemed to boil down to one concern—debts. They believed angrily that current British and French debt moratoriums comprised a dastardly slap in Uncle Sam's face. The failures of the Young and Dawes plans to bring satisfactory debt service seemed to have exacerbated and prolonged individual suffering. With President Hoover (and apparently Roosevelt at this point), most people did not think that by draining the wealth of Europe through continuing reparations/debt payments the United States made it more and more impossible for American goods to find profitable foreign markets. Old isolationist ideas were slow to die, and average Americans could not begin to understand how a foreign problem could effect the ability to earn an honest living.

As 1933 dawned, no one dared say anything about forgetting the war debts even though it became increasingly apparent that the debtor nations' abilities to pay had reached the point of no return. Even so, many salved their thoughts on the matter with a belief that the loans had been unwise and therefore instructive. Bishop James E. Freeman told his congregation in the Washington Cathedral to "learn that intergovernmental debts incurred for destructive rather than productive purposes are harmful to debtor and creditor alike." He rejected isolationism and called for complete worldwide cooperation in combating the Great Depression.[30] A minister at the First Congregational Church echoed Freeman in a sermon entitled "The Damnation of Debts."[31] It was thus easy to be sorry that the debts existed, but such publications as William Randolph Hearst's "America First" *New York American* flailed daily at Europe's beastly audacity as if to make certain that politicians got no ideas about letting those ill-begotten debts go by the board. In the old universe, no obligation was more solemn than a government debt.

January 1, 1933, dawned upon more than a half million other Americans, however, to whom "foreign debts" meant something entirely different from the war obligations of Europe. In Cessna, Pennsylvania, for example, W. E. Heltzel surveyed the prospects of 1933 and wondered if the $14,000 worth of European bonds he had purchased in 1922 would ever be worth a dime.[32] And an old fellow named H. J. Becker got up that morning in Lincoln, Nebraska, pondering a similar sorrow. He had sold his bakery as he prepared for retirement, and then sunk the proceeds, thousands of dollars, into German and Latin American bonds now in complete default. As he faced the new year, he found his savings tied up in seemingly worthless foreign bonds. In his despair, he believed "that the Wall Street bankers are back of this deal to bolster a loss they knew was coming." His thoughts turned bitterly to Washington. "Is our Government going to stand by and let these countries fleece the American people out of their hard-earned savings for which many have sacrificed the pleasures of life to save and fit themselves for a comfortable old age," he wondered, "and after all have to be the subject of charity by reason of these countries trying to evade payment of their honest debts?"[33]

In a similar quandary were Mr. and Mrs. G. P. Gullion of Carrollton, Kentucky, an Ohio River village halfway between Cincinnati and Louisville. Gullion, now seventy-three, and his father-in-law had invested everything they made from their farming operation into 8 percent Brazilian and 7 percent Bolivian bonds. They had received no interest payments on these bonds for some time; they felt that the Hoover administration misrepresented them; and they could only hope that under Mr. Roosevelt, the State Department would "stand back of these bonds."[34] By the end of 1933, more than $1.7 billion in foreign bonds were in default in the United States, representing some 190 issues guaranteed by various governments. Private citizens, institutions such as colleges, and holding organizations had most of the issues, a serious situation in anyone's estimation.

Along with millions of other American people and institutions in various categories of lost investments, individuals who held foreign bonds had fallen victim to a national disease of speculation. It had become, as

John Kenneth Galbraith observed, central to American culture. And as with so many other problems, the holocaust of depression had transformed the malady into a terminal illness amid the bewilderment and despair of the afflicted. No longer would the myths that had sustained the old order of things fit the realities of the times. What Americans needed was an Old Testament prophet to come down from the mountains to outline in striking terms what needed to be done. With the foreign bond situation, complicated as it was with the inevitable difficulties of all international contracts, there was a great need for something to be done. The problem had reached Solzhenitsyn's point at which "legalistic thinking induces paralysis; it prevents one from seeing the scale and the meaning of events."[35] A cure would probably require some kind of miracle.

2

The Foreign Bond Situation, 1933

And caused me to pass by them round about:
and, behold,
there were very many in the open valley;
and, lo,
they were very dry.

As part of its final awakening as a world power during World War I, the United States passed the point at which other nations owed it more than it owed abroad, and America was suddenly a creditor nation. The bumptious economic expansion of the late nineteenth century had made this transformation inevitable, but it had not, unfortunately, prepared American people or economic institutions for this new role. "This development," observed John Foster Dulles in 1933, "found our bankers and our investing public less experienced than if the shift from debtor to creditor position had been a gradual one."[1]

By the end of World War I, massive intergovernmental loans had accumulated on the Treasury's books, and as the twenties began, private capital followed suit, flowing abroad at an accelerated rate. Banking houses believed that the American market for bonds had no saturation point, and countries willing to borrow in the United States were equal to the task.[2] A conservative estimate suggests that between 1920 and the deepening of world depression in 1931, more than $10.5 billion in foreign bonds had been floated in the United States. Originating in forty-two foreign states, these bonds came into existence under no supervision at all.[3] Many were reckless in their promises, promiscuous in distribution and amount, and possessive of imprudently high interest rates. It was only natural that with the onset of international economic troubles most of these irresponsible loans would fall into default. Indeed, by the end of 1934, some 190 issues worth more than $1 billion were in some stage of default.[4]

Holding an average of $3,000 worth of these bonds each, the approximately seven hundred thousand Americans who held foreign bonds viewed the scene with increasing despair. They had no apparent way to secure redress and no means of communication among themselves. In such an environment, a malignant suspicion grew that American investors were suffering discrimination at the hands of the debtors, and that the U.S. government would or could not help.[5] If these defaulted foreign bonds, like the dry bones in Ezekiel's valley, were to rise again to life, considerable forthtelling would be necessary.[6]

The chronicle of American private investment abroad during the twenties, with all its insanity, tells a story of unbelievably foolhardy purchases on the part of investors and irresponsible flotations on the part of foreign governments and their collaborators in the issue house establishment in the United States. It also indicates some interesting things about the mood of America in the 1920s; the causes of these poor investments were rooted in postwar overabundance and prosperity. In contrast to some of the junk stocks on the market, however, the unhealthy bonds had seemed very attractive, safe, and foolproof. Investors with small means could hardly resist the skin-deep beauty of the foreign bond offerings on the American market in the 1920s. As a result, they flocked to the foreign bond market in incredible numbers. Most issues floated literally on a sea of nickels and dimes. For example, approximately 96 percent of those who held Chilean bonds had less than $20,000 worth, with an average of only $800 per person. Many reported holdings of more than $20,000 actually represented trust accounts of small holders.[7]

The gaudy attractiveness of the weak foreign bonds should have in itself made investors wary. Many issues were simply too good to be true. Particularly inducive to an American with a few dollars to invest were the very high interest rates attached to some foreign bond issues. For example, of the 182 issues sold in the twenties that were in partial or complete default by 1935, only seven carried a promise of less than 6 percent per annum. Of the rest, twenty-three were at more than 8 percent, with the remainder at somewhere between 6 and 8 percent.[8] Domestic bonds could not hope to compete with such rates. The average interest rate on both defaulted and nondefaulted foreign bond issues of more than $10 million was 6.36 percent, compared with a domestic bond average of 5.3 percent. Significantly, when considered alone, the average interest rate on defaulted foreign issues was much higher.[9]

Most small investors of the twenties shared a belief that in addition to their exorbitant interest rates, foreign bonds were extremely safe. Surely nothing could be more honorable than the promise of a sovereign government.[10] No one seemed to notice that at least five times since the end of the Napoleonic War more than a century before a similar wave of foreign lending had "ended with at least some occurrence of repayments breakdown, sometimes because of international trade depression, sometimes because of governmental budget crises, and sometimes because of revelation of financial abuses."[11] As a matter of fact, according to one economist, "the most remarkable thing about government debts is the consistency with which they are repudiated by war, inflation, simple fiat, or the disappearance or reconstitution of the government that issued them."[12] Instead, the typical prospectus emphasized in bold type the security and protective provisions of the loan agreements. Such seemingly iron-clad guarantees as revenue pledges and mortgages of national property appeared reassuringly in advertising. Unfortunately, lengthy legal gibberish accompanying the bonds that might have tipped the buyer to weaknesses in the issues was most often indecipherable and obscure even to the few small investors who read it. It was therefore impossible for them to see anything except the highly touted but unrealistic security and protective clauses.[13]

Although the blame in the old laissez-faire universe fell like a collapsing brick wall upon the unwise investor, other culprits had been all too willing to take advantage of such impetuousness. U.S. bankers had shown themselves incredibly inept at the foreign bond business that suddenly mushroomed after World War I. There had no doubt been a considerable lack of experience, but that could not excuse the many cases of chicanery, recklessness, and outright ignorance on the part of bankers. Amazingly enough, most of them did not even see the desirability of coordinating their lending activities with existing commercial and trade policies, something of disasterous portent even without world depression.[14] Simply stated, the old god Competition had blinded American bankers in the foreign bond business. Bankers often became so anxious to create business that they paid "finders' fees" on occasion to foreign officials or their relatives for originating new issues. In addition, with various houses competing for the right to write the bonds, foreign governments could bargain favorably on the amount and terms for the loan. Many bankers even sought to induce foreign governments to accept unsolicited loans. "Naturally it is a tempting thing," said one financier, "for certain governments to find a horde of American bankers sitting on their doorsteps offering them money."[15] The availability of anxious speculators and their money in the United States thus created an unhealthy lenders' market that inevitably could bring only catastrophe.

Bankers, surveying in the early thirties the wreckage of defaulted bonds, tended naturally to excuse themselves from culpability, as they would again in the 1980s.[16] They contended that most of their mistakes had little to do with the defaults,[17] but they could hardly deny the accuracy of an indictment that a Senate committee returned against them in 1934: "The record of the activities of investment bankers in the flotation of foreign securities is one of the most scandalous chapters in the history of American investment banking. The sale of these foreign issues was characterized by practices and abuses which were violative of the most elementary principles of business ethics."[18] The senators cited the financial community for its failure to "exercise discrimination" on eight counts of its involvement in the foreign bond business.

[They] failed to check adequately the information furnished by foreign officials, ignored bad debt records and bad moral risks; disregarded political disturbances and upheavals; failed to examine, or examined only perfunctorily, economic conditions in foreign countries; failed to determine whether the proposed uses of the proceeds of loan issues were genuinely constructive; failed to ascertain whether revenues pledged for the service of loans were collected and properly deposited in accordance with the agreements; and generally indulged in practices of doubtful propriety in the promotion of foreign loans and in the sale of foreign securities to the American public.[19]

Although the bankers might successfully have challenged the relationship of their practices to the subsequent defaults, there can be little doubt that they indulged in some careless and often unscrupulous activities. If nothing else, their behavior had encouraged the expansion of unwise investments in inherently shaky foreign bond issues.

Perhaps the most untoward practice of the issue houses lay in the cultivation of an unsound investment psychology. They taught the public to depend upon the security and protective provisions of the loan agreements rather than to check the paying capacity and reliability of the debtor country.[20] Men and women of modest means would certainly concern themselves with safety before they committed their funds, but with misleading and actually worthless provisions so prominent in prospectuses and advertising, they understandably failed to look deeper for real indicators of safety. The investment bankers consciously played upon this factor. They first failed to draft bonds that provided against all major risks, and then they magnified the "secured loan" claim, undoubtedly to soothe the suspicions of prospective buyers who might not have accepted bonds from a country they knew nothing about. In reality, most of the security provisions were virtually worthless in that they usually amounted in essence only to additional promises as easily breakable as the one that brought the default.[21] As one investment firm official admitted, "the pledges of revenues [and mortgages, etc.] are not worth the paper they are written on, on foreign loans."[22] Most damning is that bankers surely knew from the outset that the pledges were worthless even as they emphasized them. They knew, for example, that the only effective security on a foreign bond comes when a creditor power has control over the customs collections of the debtor. Between 1916 and 1937 in Haiti, for example, a general receiver (nominated by the president of the United States) collected revenues, and full bond service continued.[23]

When hard times came, a natural vulnerability for all international loans followed, but those with already shaky foundations were almost automatically doomed to default, especially those that had done nothing to bolster the national economy of the borrower. This was particularly true of many of the Latin American issues. Because nations with the poorest credit ratings had to promise higher interest payments to secure loans, their bonds had virtually no chance of avoiding default with a disruption of the international economy. As the trade restrictions of the world depression increased, underdeveloped nations generally found themselves unable to secure enough dollars through exports to meet high interest and principal payments.[24] Compounding the problem of the decline in foreign trade was a worsening endemic inability to obtain foreign exchange. Many debtor governments were able to continue debt service with internal revenues, but only if measured in the debtor's own currency. When they were unable to buy American dollars, they had no choice but to declare their bonds as in default.[25] Hence, "the inability to pay" often meant more than a simple lack of funds to be applied to debt service.

Many embittered American investors (like H. J. Becker in chapter 1) believed that there was more voluntary withholding of debt service than "inability to pay," and there may have been something to that belief in many cases. Debtors often convinced themselves as times grew worse that the way in which the issue houses had handled their bonds excused debtors' responsibilities to bondholders. Thus they looked upon the bankers' actions for an easement of conscience as they announced defaults. After all, unsavory circumstances attending issuance could not have avoided coloring debtors' views toward their bond obligations. Also, the unrepresentative character of many of those Latin American governments may have been a factor, especially where such governments were ousted by force in 1930 and 1931.[26] It became a delightfully simple matter to argue, as had the postrevolutionary government of France in 1792, that "the sovereignty of peoples is not bound by the treaties of tyrants."[27] In other cases, however, borrowers understandably pushed debt service low on their list of national priorities and simply used available revenue to provide for national exigencies. Certainly the examples of parallel intergovernmental debt suspensions, the apparent death of the gold standard, and deepening depression encouraged many debtors to consider defaulting to private citizens as an acceptable answer to their internal financial difficulties. As evidence of this, many borrower states refused to rectify defaults, even after they had declared their ability to pay restored.[28] Nevertheless, most defaulting debtors explained their action sincerely, citing a real dearth of revenue and available foreign exchange. And in almost all cases, especially in those in which a state borrowed far beyond its means and needs, depression, decline in world trade, and a general drop in prices made defaults practically inevitable.[29] This all may have seemed like a "fleecing" to the Beckers of America, but to many besieged and unstable governments, default to faceless foreign nationals promised a relatively painless easing of local financial problems.

Trapped in the troubled present of the disastrous epoch of the 1930s, creditors and debtors alike could not see over the edges of the deep hole in which they found themselves uncomfortably together. They could not comprehend the complex currents pulling upon the international economy, nor the changes in the world order that had emerged from the holocaust of the Great War. No longer present, for example, was the stabilizing force of an immutable gold standard, backed by sterling British domination of the international monetary system.[30] And although foreign lending became a giddy fad among Americans in the 1920s, the United States was ill-prepared to replace Britain as the bulwark of the international economy. Even laissez-faire champion Herbert Hoover could not persuade financiers to accede to a policy of government review of foreign lending as a modest first step in recognizing the magnitude of American involvement in the lending wave of the twenties.[31]

Financial innovation stepped gingerly past such heretical ideas to take advantage of a new American familiarity with the merits of foreign bonds engendered by the Liberty Loan campaign.[32] In order to create a market for all this potential investment capital, the bankers, as we have seen, literally stumbled over themselves to persuade foreign governments to borrow American money. "It was said at the time that the leading hotels in Germany had a very prosperous time because most of their rooms were taken by representatives of American financial houses who came to Germany to persuade some obscure municipality to accept a large loan."[33] Other countries, particularly in Latin America, encountered similarly irresponsible temptors, but the war-crippled Germans seemed a most tantalizing target. Even so, Reichsbank President Hjalman Schacht tried heroically to stem the tide of foreign capital flooding his country in the late twenties, noting that much of it was going to such improvements as municipal swimming pools that would in no way contribute to Germany's ability to obtain the foreign exchange necessary to repay the loans.[34]

In Latin America, where borrowed capital also disappeared typically into similarly unhealthy squanderings, a more serious condition arose as some governments began to use the new easy money "to retire previous debts, to prevent default on existing loans, or to cover domestic deficits."[35] In 1928 and 1929, short-term borrowing by foreign governments accelerated dramatically, most of it to cover interest payments on long-term loans. Debtors had thus begun to reveal just how heavily addicted to regular injections of foreign capital they had become. Inevitably, the crash of the securities market in the fall of 1929 left such "loan junkies" high and dry.[36] But from the perspective of debtors thus afflicted, the people who pushed the loans appeared much more liable than the addicts for the resultant cost of the ensuing economic dysfunction. Latin American scholars in particular have challenged the classic creditor views that debt crises emerge largely because of policy errors on the part of debtor governments and that trade liberalization and direct foreign investment allow debtors to grow out of their indebtedness. Such contentions, scholars argue, simply encourage more dependence upon foreign capital.[37] Instead, boom-and-bust debt cycles result primarily from fluctuations in the world economy—fluctuations over which borrowers have little control—and from cases where foreign loan negotiations become powerful political tools with extensive social and economic ramifications.[38] In such a view, indebtedness shows itself to be "a central circular mechanism within the numerous vicious circles of underdevelopment, . . . one of its causes or at least one of the principal means by which it perpetuates itself."[39] The American economist Albert Fishlow put it perhaps more succinctly: "In the last analysis, the debt problem is a development problem, not one of liquidity or solvency or even of the vulnerability of the financial system."[40]

Whatever its cosmic nature, U.S. investment abroad at the time of the stock market crash of 1929 totaled some $15.4 billion. That figure equals nearly 95 billion 1984 dollars, more than the amount of American bank claims on developing countries at the time of the foreign debt crash of 1982. In 1929, however, the bulk of the paper languished in the hands of bondholders, primarily families and businesses, rather than on the balance sheets of banks.[41] Perhaps the greatest difficulties in dealing with the foreign bond situation stemmed from a lack of understanding at all levels of the nature of foreign security in general, what laws it obeyed (if any), and to which stimuli it would respond.[42] It was easy to confuse foreign securities with domestic bonds and to assume they were the same creature, or perhaps cousins from abroad. In reality, there were few similarities, especially with regard to redress on a default. In the foreign bond situation, all bondholders had to either accept an agreement on readjustment or receive nothing. No court existed that could have effective jurisdiction, due to a foreign government's immunity from suit without its consent—"no judicial scrutiny or supervision of either the activities of those who negotiate for the holders . . . or the plan of readjustment which they negotiate."[43]

In general, two documents were incident to a foreign bond issue: the loan contract between the debtor and the house of issue, and the fiscal agency's agreement with the debtor. The house of issue and the fiscal agency were generally closely related. The loan was issued on "full faith and credit" with a mortgage or revenue allocation pledge in an extremely detailed contract. With a domestic bond, such covenants would have been effective because of legal recourse in the event of default, but in a foreign bond they were just so many words.[44] All sides had to accept voluntarily any arrangement arrived at through negotiation and compromise. In any case, no legal machinery existed that could collect a judgment.[45] Even document mortgages were fairly useless in the legal sense, because a debtor's courts had jurisdiction; the property was usually essential to the debtor citizenry, such as a government-owned power plant; and surely any foreign state would have regarded an attempt at foreclosure as interference with its sovereignty and an affront to its dignity.[46] Without doubt there were states whose national courts might have granted a creditor relief, but unfortunately these were the countries in which no suit was necessary. A public loan was an act of sovereignty, as was its suspension or repudiation, that bound the national courts.[47]

The problem facing almost three-quarters of a million Americans who held foreign bonds as the depression deepened had thus reached perplexing proportions. It seemed that only two forces existed with enough resources and comprehension to provide possible relief: the banking houses that sold the securities and the American government.[48] As for the bankers, certainly many felt an actual "moral responsibility" to people to whom they had sold the now-defaulted bonds. However, less commendable motives frequently impelled their actions on a default case. For example, bankers often held short-term credits on the defaulting government, and continuing service on these was of far more importance than redress for unhappy bond customers. Sometimes in issuing a particular security there had been fraud or negligence that bankers were not anxious to have revealed. Often, bankers were more worried about future business with debtors, or their image to obligors, than they were about acting forcefully on a defaulted issue.[49] Consequently, the involvement of bankers in readjustment efforts developed into a vice comparable to that in which they had indulged during the sale of the securities.[50] It followed that the bewildered bondholders, sensing that their bankers were accomplishing little in their behalf, and in keeping with the psychology of the New Deal, turned to government. Surely Washington would not stand by while foreign powers fleeced Americans.

Most bondholders did not understand the grave and complex problems in international relations attending any contemplated attempt on the part of the government to become involved in the defaulted foreign bond situation. Basically, government assistance might proceed along three possible avenues: economic sanctions, the use of armed force, and diplomatic representation. All were fraught with tremendous difficulties, but the first two were out of the question at the time. The use of economic weapons was not a part of American international policy in the thirties, and it is doubtful whether such methods as discriminatory tariffs and regulation of foreign exchange would have accomplished anything for creditors given the tenor of the times. As the Securities and Exchange Commission later noted, "Their natural tendency to cripple commerce and to equalize trade between the two nations may make the sanction itself ineffective."[51] As for the rare creditor displays of armed force, other issues usually helped to spur deployment. A prime example occurred in 1903 when Venezuela refused to submit to arbitration tort claims. Growing out of that situation, the so-called Drago Doctrine[51] subsequently led to a "Convention Respecting the Limitation of the Employment of Force for the Recovery of Contract Debts" at the Second Hague Conference, an agreement that outlawed armed intervention to collect debts except when the debtor (1) ignores an arbitration offer, (2) obstructs the framing of an accepted arbitration agreement, or (3) fails to submit an arbitrated reward.[53]

The third, more feasible approach to governmental assistance, diplomatic representation, was more complex and multifaceted. International lawyers generally believed that outright diplomatic intervention could legally occur only in cases of "delinquency," or when a debtor openly repudiated the obligation (which happened rarely) as opposed to the mere failure to service it. A government might also justify diplomatic intervention if it believed that the debtor was practicing discrimination against particular creditors—"the difference between repudiation and discriminatory treatment on the one hand, and ordinary default on the other."[54] Hence, diplomatic representation on the part of the United States occasionally took the form of mild protests and requests for rectification, but more often Washington acted informally by letting debtors know of its interests and desires regarding a particular default situation.

Because national and international considerations transcended in importance the immediate interest of bondholders, the State Department most frequently moved guardedly if at all in its representations in behalf of persons who held foreign securities.[55] But such reluctance only lent support to those who blamed the State Department for tacitly approving the bond buying in the first place. In response to such feelings, the Democratic National Platform of 1932 contained the following plank: "We condemn the usurpation of power by the State Department in assuming to pass upon foreign securities offered by international bankers, as a result of which billions of dollars in questionable bonds have been sold to the public upon the implied approval of the Federal Government."[56] Thus, while not wanting to appear "as Shylock before the whole debtor world,"[57] politicians and government functionaries recognized that for the first time in American history, the protection of bondholders had become a major factor in its international relations and a major problem in the path to world recovery.[58]

The plight of the American bondholder in 1933 was therefore a miserable one, but nothing new in world history. The British, the French, the Belgians, and others had long been in the business of holding foreign bonds, many of which had gone into default in years past much as they were doing during the current difficulty. These countries had handled their problems. The British, for example, had until 1930 managed to readjust through sheer doggedness all defaults they had taken in hand, except those of the states of the United States. Britain's solution was in a quasi-official central bondholders' organization that could deal authoritatively with the obligations of defaulting debtors. The organization had the government's full cooperation and sanction, but it was not an official government agency and so could act forcefully with fewer repercussions in international affairs.[59] Before the inauguration of Franklin Roosevelt in 1933, such concerned foreign policy hands as Herbert Feis had begun to believe that such an organization was just what American bondholders needed. "While relenting in our efforts to collect on foreign debts due the American government," Feis recalled, "we took steps to salvage the defaulted private loans of American investors by . . . organizing a disinterested and independent organization."[60] Perhaps the miraculous would occur.

3

Divining the Miracle

And he said unto me,
Son of man, can these bones live?
And I answered,
O Lord God, thou knowest.

Early in the return to normalcy of the 1920s, State Department officials recognized the need for some control in the burgeoning foreign bond business, a remarkable thing given the then-current enthronement of laissez-faire. Secretary of State Charles Evans Hughes called a group of bankers to Washington in the summer of 1921 and requested that they consult the department on all proposed loans abroad. There followed a State Department "Rule of March 3, 1922" informing bankers that the secretary would offer his opinion on any projected loan, but that the department would "not pass upon the merits of foreign loans as business propositions, nor assume any responsibility whatever in connection with loan transactions."[1] Despite this appended caution, whenever the department "passed upon" a foreign deal as not detrimental to the political interests of the United States, the public (with the help of the security's promoters who usually mentioned the State Department action) believed that this meant the deal was therefore commercially promising and the investment a good one. Between 1922 and 1929, the department objected only rarely to private loans to foreign governments. When objection did arise, it usually resulted from one of three conditions: (1) the country seeking the loan had not refunded its war debt; (2) proceeds of the loan would be used for military purposes; and (3) proceeds of the loan would promote a monopoly of raw products needed in the United States. There were many times when the feelings of the State Department on a particular loan effected the sales of bonds much more than such valuable indicators as the circulars of the Finance and Investment Division of the Bureau of Foreign and Domestic Commerce issued from the Department of Commerce.[2]

As some of the loans it had "passed upon" began to fall into default with the onset of depression, the department vociferously disclaimed any responsibility. Two schools of nasty criticism arose, however. Senator Carter Glass led the first, chiding the department for being involved at all. A typical Glass resolution passed in the Senate on February 26, 1931: "It is the sense of the Senate that the Department of State . . . should desist from the dangerous practice of involving the United States Government in any responsibility of whatever nature, either by approval or disapproval, for foreign investment loans floated in this country."[3] The other school, whose chief protagonist was the noted international lawyer Charles Cheney Hyde, blasted the department for its failure to be *more* involved in the protection of bondholders.[4] President Hoover and Secretary of State Henry Stimson thus received fire from both sides, and as the default problem worsened, the more difficult it became to decide what course of action to pursue. Recognizing the trauma the situation was causing Stimson, Herbert Feis sent the secretary a memorandum early in 1932 outlining the British solution—a quasi-official central bondholders' council that could effectively employ "the arts which had induced debtors to pay what they fairly could without creating animosity."[5] Stimson was impressed. In April, he instructed Feis and Assistant Secretary Harvey H. Bundy, Jr., to proceed with the organization of a similar American council.[6]

Something more than the insistence of aggrieved bondholders and the presence of a ready model was spurring Stimson to action. A plethora of individuals and organizations clamored for the right to represent the bondholders. Many were sincere and capable, but most were opportunists who saw in the defaulted bondholders' plight a chance to turn a few dollars in the way of fees and commissions paid for their representations. Some of these persons and groups were blatantly dishonest, and still others were unqualified and bereft of influence. Like vultures gathering around bones, they threatened an unpleasant experience both for the anxious bondholders and for American relations with the defaulting governments. Almost weekly it seemed, new "protective committees" came into being, accelerating in number proportionate to the incidence of new defaults. By the end of 1934, more than forty such groups claimed to represent 197 issues; some were in competition on the same defaulted bonds.[7] The public was confused, and so were the debtor governments.

These protective organizations generally fell into three categories. First, firms that had floated a particular defaulted issue often established machinery to negotiate for a readjustment. Second, it was common for so-called "independent" committees to seek to represent bondholders on a specific issue, or for those of a particular country. Third, enterprising individuals set up a few "permanent" protective committees that claimed to represent all or a large portion of holders of defaulted securities. Most of the committees legitimized themselves by claiming authority from the deposit of bonds or the power of attorney from bondholders. Others did neither, and hence had no legitimate claim to legal representation.[8]

Of the three types of protective committees that multiplied in the spring of 1932, the "permanent" ones had the most bearing upon the task Feis and Bundy faced. Apparently, the first American protective committee of this sort came into existence in December 1873. Called the American Council of Bondholders, it concerned itself only with railroad securities and disappeared after a short time.[9] Then the Investment Bankers Association formed a short-lived Committee on Foreign Securities in the fall of 1918,[10] and with the Great Depression came several more, the most noticeable of which were the Latin American Bondholders Association and the American Council of Foreign Bondholders. The initiative for the latter two came from private interests; both failed.

The Latin American Bondholders Association (LABA) incorporated under the laws of New York on October 1, 1931.[11] Its motivating force was one T. F. Lee of the investment brokerage firm F. J. Lisman Company. The announced purpose of the LABA was to disseminate accurate information to set up protective committees on specific issues. After sinking $19,000 into it himself, Lee was able to obtain only an additional $515 from membership dues. He tried to get support from a foundation and, failing this, withdrew after only three months' activity. Then Montgomery Schyler (former minister to El Salvador), LABA's most prominent member, resigned. Afterward, an individual named Fred Lavis became president and continued the organization from his own pocket. Lavis was interested primarily in the title "President of the Latin American Bondholders Association" so he could gain publicity for his other efforts, including membership on a committee set up by Seligman's, another investment brokerage firm. He claimed to have a going operation with two committees (El Salvador and Colombia), but the LABA was dead in reality when Lee abandoned it. What continued as the LABA was just Lavis himself.[12]

The other enterprise came into existence at the hands of Max Winkler, an investments dealer in New York who had long urged the formation of an American counterpart to the British Council of Foreign Bondholders.[13] Unable to get governmental action, he set up his own American Council of Foreign Bondholders (ACFB) in July 1931 under the laws of Delaware. Winkler gained the support of three friends in the investment business, and eventually a few brokerage firms endorsed his efforts. He then reincorporated the ACFB in New York in November 1931, with his three friends owning 90 percent of the stock, and a group called Analyst Associates (of which Winkler was a member) holding the remaining 10 percent.[14] Strictly a profit-making operation, it excluded all but purchasers and sellers of foreign securities. Only about ninety persons subscribed to the ACFB's information circular at $25 (regular) to $100 (special) a year, with as little as $3 acceptable. The ACFB also claimed to be setting up committees on specific issues, but never really did so. Winkler asserted that the group was the American version of the British council, a similarity that actually existed in name only. The ACFB's only real role was in the dissemination of investment advice, whereas the British group offered none. In addition, ACFB's advice was available only to subscribers; the BCFB distributed its counsel to the press. The inner circle of ACFB was comprised of brokers, whose livelihood depended upon buying and selling the very securities to which their advice related.[15]

In addition to Lavis and Winkler, a third type of individual conspired to become involved, simply to reap some of the windfall from the defaulted foreign bond situation. Lawrence E. de S. Hoover represented the archetype of a very careless sort who formed committees with no particular reference on the part of the members to the ownership or representation of securities, or to members' skill, experience, or training in the foreign bond field. Returning unemployed from a trip to Colombia, Hoover struck upon the idea of forming a committee for holders of Colombian bonds as a possibly lucrative entrepreneurial activity. Gaining attention by attacking the banking houses and investment brokers, whom he said were afraid of his work, he managed to obtain the confidence (and money) of a number of distressed bondholders.[16] The bankers reciprocated his attacks, maintaining that "the readjustment of issues which have defaulted is the prerogative of the bankers who had placed the issue."[17] Hoover's activities bore tragicomic results in other respects as well. For instance, he claimed to be acting "at the request of a number of the holders," when, as it later developed, he knew only two of them. He also said that his committee members held bonds, a complete fabrication. In truth, he had selected his "core" from a group that happened to be having lunch at the India House in New York, where Hoover and a friend were discussing formation of the committee.[18]

Such was the scene in the spring of 1932 as Fcis and Bundy went about their charge of creating a responsible, governmentally sanctioned bond-holders' protective council. The two men wrestled with several problems, the foremost of which was finding trustworthy and disinterested persons on whom the State Department and the bondholders could rely to gain expertise and exercise sound judgment. In the best of circumstances, that was a high order. Also perplexing was the question of adequate financing without dependence upon the Treasury or the banks, as well as the difficulty of securing the cooperation of the jealous and suspicious financial community.[19] The activities of such men as Hoover, Lavis, and Winkler only increased the difficulty of the job.

The State Department officials, in cooperation with the Department of Treasury, found seven private citizens to join with various government officers at an April 15, 1932, meeting in Washington to discuss the increasing defaults and the possible formation of a central protective committee. The distinguished group that assembled included Treasury Secretary Ogden Mills, Assistant Secretary William R. Castle, Feis and Bundy from State, Grosvenor M. Jones of Commerce, Yale University law professor and member of the Council on Foreign Relations Charles P. Howland, Chairman Pierre Jay of the Fiduciary Trust Co. of New York, Princeton University professor Edwin Kemmerer, and attorneys Thomas N. Perkins of Boston and George Rublee of Washington, D.C.[20] Noting that the defaults at that moment amounted to about $800 million, the State Department people recounted the many inquiries that were haunting them and added that many people were accusing the department of nonfeasance. They also discussed the "racket" condition of lawyers, bankers, and charlatans who created reorganization committees.[21]

The group agreed that although the government could take the proper initiative in a movement to form a central council, private citizens would have to take the responsibility. "It seemed rather obvious to us," recalled

Rublee, "that the Council to act in a disinterested way should be a company of men who never had anything to do with the issue of the bonds."[22] Consequently, a committee composed of Howland, Jay, Kemmerer, Perkins, Rublee (all of whom had been at the meeting) and former Ambassador to Germany Alanson B. Houghton submitted a report under the leadership of Howland and Rublee to the Department of State on May 23, 1932. The committee recommended a council of fifteen eminent men, to be established on the general model of the British organization.[23]

Not wanting to estrange the banking houses at the outset, the committee hedged somewhat on the degree of power it would confer upon the council. "The Council should, in the Committee's opinion, intervene directly only in emergencies or affairs of great importance where more authority and prestige were necessary."[24] The committee also had serious doubts about whether an American council could handle the situation as fluidly as the British one, inasmuch as it believed that "the American banking community was not as homogeneous and closely knit as the British, nor were its members as trustful."[25] Characteristic of the corporate ideals the organizers brought to the task, the committee wanted to keep the bankers' feet to the fire. "The one thought that we had from the very start," Jay remembered, "was that the house of issue in case of defaulted bonds had a distinct moral responsibility toward the proposed bondholders, and that nothing in the formation of this proposed body should relieve them one whit of their responsibility."[26]

Approving the report, Secretary Stimson asked the group on June 2 to proceed with the selection of personnel and to discover methods of finance for the council. Ominously, at least one member of the department, Feis himself, had already become worried that the committee had given the bankers too much deference. Confiding to Stimson his concern that the bankers might not always put bondholders' interest above their own, Feis questioned "whether they had retained the confidence of many of those who had bought the bonds, or the good will of some of the defaulters."[27] Some question also arose about whether the chief banking houses (often rival creditors with the bondholders) might be guilty of conflict of interest if encouraged from the council to continue to form protective committees. Subsequently, Stimson and Mills recommended to the organizers that the council "should play a primary and independent part in representing the bondholders and not merely serve as a coordinating agency for committees sponsored by the bankers."[28]

By the end of October 1932, the Hoover administration had approved definite plans for an American bondholders' council, but other election-year priorities quickly buried the problem,[29] even though the default question and the role of the State Department had become an issue in the presidential campaign. Hoover and Stimson, of course, defended their policy and those of their Republican predecessors.[30] Roosevelt, in typical fashion, changed his mind on the issue daily, first taking the Hyde position,[31] then Glass's.[32] He eventually settled on the position that the government should tell the public of bad investments, but not good ones.[33] Continuing to speak disdainfully of foreign lending, Roosevelt often implied that the Hoover administration was somehow responsible for the current plight of the bondholders. Undoubtedly, the Democrats saw a political boon in the foreign bond issue; throughout the campaign, they emphasized incorrectly that Republican State Departments had "passed upon the financial soundness" of the defaulted issues. Concomitantly, they carefully neglected to mention that the department had made it clear that it was approving an issue's acceptability only upon considerations of the national interest.[34]

After the Democratic victory in November, some doubt arose because of what Roosevelt had said during the campaign about whether he would follow through with the bondholders' council project.[35] Meanwhile, Congress acted on the problem by melding Senator Hiram Johnson's Corporation of Foreign Bondholders Bill into the proposed Securities Act as Title II. The Johnson Amendment, as it was known in the administration, provided for an organization that would have been virtually an agency of the government, financed with federal funds and run indirectly by the Federal Trade Commission.[36] Happily for those favoring some other arrangement, Senator Ben Cohen (a James M. Landis protégé) managed to attach a "saving clause" to the bill, reserving to the president the right to delay its execution until he "decides its taking effect is in the public interest."[37]

Worried about the fate of the efforts of 1932, Feis submitted a lengthy memorandum to incoming Secretary of State Cordell Hull on March 15, 1933. He reported that the organizing group (of April 1932) had met in December with members of the banking industry who assured the proposed council "the right connections," and that they had settled upon a general board of directors. "Mr. George Rublee . . . and Mr. Allen Dulles, who has been assisting the committee, reported to me yesterday that they believed they could see the end of the road," Feis wrote. "The plans and personalities seem to us excellent and . . . we trust that the council will come into actual existence very shortly."[38] Rublee and Dulles came to the department that same day to get assurances that the plans and personalities were entirely agreeable to the government. They hoped that by doing so "there will be established between the council and the Department friendly relationships."[39] When Undersecretary William Phillips later discussed the matter with Roosevelt, the president showed himself entirely in favor of the Feis plan over the Johnson Amendment.[40] Obviously, FDR never intended to institute the Title II corporation, even though he continued to let everyone believe that he was "debating" the advisability of putting it into being.[41] Some evidence suggests that presidential aides Henry Morgenthau and Louis Howe purposefully put forth this notion to curry favor with Johnson and Title II's House supporter Sam Rayburn.[42]

The longer they delayed announcing their decision on the matter, the more Roosevelt and his advisors became convinced that the Johnson Amendment was a bad idea. The more they considered Title II, the longer the list of objections became. (1) The corporation would be more responsible than the State Department in the foreign investments field, a potentially embarrassing situation. (2) There would be a conflict of interest when a debtor owed both the United States and its citizens. (3) Political pressure in a government corporation would be too great. (4) Corporation statistics (necessarily vague) would be considered official and accurate. (5) Progress in settling defaults would be very slow, and no administration would want the blame for seeming inactive.[43] In addition, the brokerage community continued to argue that only the experts (the bankers) could deal with the problem effectively. "Bankruptcy is an emergency which requires action," wrote Lisman. "Democracy is generally too much like a debating society."[44]

From the other side, other cries denounced as "absurd" Roosevelt's "delay" in putting Title II into effect.[45] The president shrewdly played the waiting game until it could appear that he had decided at the last moment "that it would be better to create an agency with similar functions but divorced from such a close relationship with the Government."[46] When the Securities Act of 1933 (with Title II) passed in May and became law with Roosevelt's signature, the public ignored the "saving clause" and assumed that the Corporation of Foreign Bondholders would soon come into existence.[47] This was the signal for which Lavis and Winkler had been waiting. Both hoped that the State Department would use their respective organizations as the nucleus for the Title II organization. Winkler even went so far as to reincorporate his ACFB into a nonprofit organization and to draft a bill for submission to Congress authorizing the president to declare ACFB as the government's corporation for holders of foreign bonds.[48] But beneath the surface, the small organizing group, at work now for more than a year, pressed forward through the summer in its efforts to launch the private corporation.[49]

Late in the spring, the German government announced a suspension of payments on all external bonds. After John Foster Dulles left for Europe in his capacity as a partner in the firm of Sullivan and Cromwell to negotiate on the default, pressure mounted on Roosevelt to set up the Title II corporation.[50] He continued to stall. Then, at the end of July, he held a highly publicized meeting with Charles H. March, chair of the Federal Trade Commission, to discuss the "Corporation of Foreign Security Holders" question. Afterward, he issued the following statement to the press:

> Almost everybody in the country with as much as $1000 in his pocket either has actually paid good money for a foreign bond which has later proved worthless in view of the means formerly available for forcing a collection, or has at sometime or another been on the verge of falling into such a trap.
>
> Now we are going right after that kind of thing with a vengeance which has already been delayed too long. I want it put strongly that something is now going to happen that will bring the American money back to American agriculture and industry, where it belongs.[51]

On August 3, Roosevelt met with Raymond Stevens, another member of the Federal Trade Commission, to discuss the issue. Stevens had been an early and vigorous opponent of Title II. Just a few days before this meeting, he had written the president, "I am, as a Democrat, seriously concerned to see your administration assume an obligation under Title II for a situation which occurred under Republican rule, and for which you are in no sense responsible."[52] At the conclusion of his meeting with Stevens, Roosevelt refused comment.[53] At this point, however, it was becoming increasingly obvious because of his inaction that the president had in mind not Title II but rather a private group. In any case, it seemed that time was wasting. The Montevideo Conference of Inter-American States, where the debt question would surely arise, was fast approaching, and the default situation was growing worse daily. By the end of September, experts estimated that nearly $2 billion worth of foreign bonds were in default in the United States, more than double the amount of just a year before. Perhaps, speculated one newspaper, "the President and his advisers hesitate to raise in the hearts of hundreds of thousands of voters hopes which might prove illusory."[54]

What the public did not know was that Roosevelt had definitely decided by the end of August to move ahead with the private organization for bondholders.[55] The council had not come into existence simply because its organizing group, at work now for seventeen months, had been unable to move faster on the solution of its immediate problems of finance, personnel, and bylaws. The process finally all but completed, Roosevelt discussed the formation of the council on October 6 with Hull, March, and Treasury Undersecretary Dean Acheson.[56] With these meetings came much speculation in the press about what was in the offing. Gone was the illusion that Title II would see reality; by October 17, reporters had learned that the committee would nevertheless have government sanction and no members who had "passed upon loans or who had investment advisory work." The papers had also chosen either Newton Baker or James M. Cox as the director.[57] Shortly thereafter, Roosevelt's choice for director, Raymond Stevens (former Minister to Siam), met with Hull, Acheson, and the president.[58] At that meeting, Roosevelt gave Stevens the go-ahead for the creation of the council. He had to turn down a disgruntled Senator Johnson, but he believed that his action was both "courageous and wise."[59]

Accordingly, Stevens prepared letters of invitation for "eighteen prominent gentlemen" to come to Washington to hear the plans for the organization and to agree to become its first board of directors. Under the signatures of Hull, March, and Treasury Secretary William Woodin, the letters went out on October 13, 1933.[60] On the twentieth, a Friday, fifteen of those carefully invited individuals met in the Federal Reserve Board offices in the Treasury Building with officials of the State Department and the Federal Trade Commission. They heard the details of their proposed service and then moved the conference into the White House, where President Roosevelt joined them and secured their agreement "to take upon them the patriotic duty of bringing into existence an adequate, effective and disinterested organization to carry on . . . the settlement of private [international] debt situations."[61]

Even with the careful groundwork, this was no mean achievement for the president. Of the fifteen men, two were former governors of midwestern states, three were respected academicians, two were bankers, and three were former State Department principals. Nearly all were lawyers. Among the three invited who did not attend but agreed by letter to serve were the two most recognizable and respected names Stevens had sought for the council: Charles Francis Adams, former secretary of the navy, and Newton D. Baker, Wilson's secretary of war. The third absent individual was someone with whom George Rublee had worked when both were aides to Ambassador Dwight Morrow in Mexico, and who had succeeded Morrow to that post: Joshua Reuben Clark, Jr.[62]

After leaving Roosevelt's office, the conferees appointed Stevens and three others as an Organizing Committee to present, as soon as possible, a complete recommendation for the incorporation of the group. Then the conference adjourned. At once, the White House publicity corps scurried to capitalize upon the meeting, engendering the story that the president had junked Title II only after Hull had supposedly waged a dedicated campaign against it.[63] More portentous for the future, they released a lengthy statement that clearly marked the council's course along some- times impossible terrain.[64] Nevertheless, the bush was finally burning, and all the apprehensive American holders of defaulted foreign bonds could at last hope that something was going to be done, that maybe the bones could live again.

CHAPTER

4

Anointing the Prophet

Again he said unto me,
Prophesy upon these bones, and say unto them,
O ye dry bones,
hear the word of the Lord.

Loyal Democrat Raymond B. Stevens of New Hampshire was President Roosevelt's hand-picked choice to lead the American effort to revitalize the $2 billion worth of defaulted foreign bonds afloat in the United States by the end of 1933. With a long record of faithful public service, his experience in foreign affairs as a former minister to Siam and in international economics as a member of the Federal Trade Commission made Stevens a natural choice for the delicate task. Stevens would run the show. Accordingly, after the October 1933 conference, the administration felt that the problem of people who held foreign bonds was out of its hands and good riddance. Roosevelt was busy with his most radical effort—a planned economy under the National Industrial Recovery Act.[1] Secretary of State Cordell Hull worried about the recognition of the Soviet Union (which came on November 16), and about the coming Conference of Inter-American States at Montevideo at the end of December.

During the course of the council organization, Stevens had learned that the Brazilian government was willing to begin negotiations on the readjustment of its dollar debts in default since 1931 and 1932. That spring, Sir Otto Niemeyer, Stevens's British counterpart, negotiated a plan that would have provided for a general resumption of Brazilian payments. The State Department, however, expressed dissatisfaction with the Niemeyer plan because it seemed to deal with the Brazilian dollar bond issue unfairly.[2] Consequently, Stevens and Hull agreed that a member of the pending American bondholders' council should go to Rio de Janeiro to work on fair treatment for dollar bonds under a revised Niemeyer plan. Hull mentioned that he had already considered former Ambassador to Mexico J. Reuben Clark as a possible delegate to Montevideo.[3] They therefore decided that the Utah lawyer and member-designate of the council would stop in Rio on the way to and from the conference to prevail upon the Brazilians to revise the Niemeyer plan to eliminate threatened discrimination against American bondholders.[4] The work of the council would be underway before the organization actually existed. It would signal an auspicious beginning, if only Clark could find some success.

Still in front of Stevens and his organizing committee lay the problems of incorporation under adequate bylaws, the establishment of staff and offices, and the great difficulty of obtaining finances. Unfortunately, Stevens had a lingering illness that grew steadily worse as the winter deepened. He cut his activities drastically, leaving most of the work to the three other members of the committee, Hendon Chubb, Thomas Thacher, and J. C. Traphagen.[5] Not privy to the groundwork of Rublee, Feis, Stevens, and others, the three found themselves hard-pressed to bring life to the council without Stevens's full efforts. They would be at work for nearly two months. In the meantime, Clark sailed for Rio de Janeiro and Montevideo on November 11, 1933, while the other members-designate of the council began to assume responsibilities that came upon them in a frightful deluge as soon as their names appeared in the newspapers. Most of the men confessed complete unpreparedness for what befell them. Chicago attorney Laird Bell, for example, received a cabinet full of applications for positions on the council's staff within the first week after he attended the Washington meeting. With great concern, he wrote to Feis:

> To date my only activity as a member of the committee on foreign bonds had been the filing of applications for jobs. I live in fear, however, that somebody will presently ask me some questions about the situation and I can think of practically no question that I could answer. In consequence, I am wondering whether there is

some easy way I could educate myself on the general situation. By that I mean, is there any place where I can find what foreign issues have been sold in the United States in any considerable number, which are in default, who the underwriting houses are, etc.? Could you give me a lead?[6]

Bell's ignorance was not the exception but the rule. In their anxiety to gather a group devoid of connections with the investment banking establishment, the organizers had failed to recognize that such council members would be largely unable to do much besides lend their names and file letters. Mills Lane of Georgia and Traphagen were the only directors who were bankers, and even they were not engaged in the foreign investments field. Feis accordingly requested and received from the American legation in Paris a bulky dossier on the operating procedures of the various councils of other creditor nations.[7] He also distributed copies of a lengthy summary of the international bond situation (also prepared in the Paris legation) to council members.[8]

Secretary Hull, on board a ship bound for South America, became concerned toward the end of November about the long delay in the establishment of the council. The Mexican delegate Puig Casauranc had assured him that one of the major issues at Montevideo would be the debt question. Without the organization of the central committee, Hull would have nothing firm to tell the confused Latin American debtors. Most of them were extremely unhappy about the plethora of representations arriving from the multiplying number of protective committees and angry American bondholders, and it seemed that the government of the United States was doing nothing.[9] Hull consequently telegraphed the department from sea on November 28, 1933, inquiring about the slowness of progress in getting the council into operation.[10] The department's reply undoubtedly provided the secretary with a good measure of chagrin. In addition to Stevens's illness, perplexing financial problems had arisen. "A second refusal by Rockefeller Foundation was unexpected." The telegram to Hull finished pessimistically and fearfully: "Maybe we'll have to renew Title II of Securities Act to finance it if cannot get it otherwise."[11] The planners had been sure that funds would be forthcoming, particularly from the foundations. Hence, the final Rockefeller refusal landed as a severe blow.

Undaunted, the Stevens group continued to work on the problem, turning their attention to the financial institutions, especially the New

York banks and issue houses. On December 6, about twenty representatives of various banks met at the Federal Reserve Board offices in New
York at the request of one of its governors. Stevens's address presumably
was successful; most issue houses subsequently agreed to provide support
for the council. Pierre Jay spoke on the same day to a meeting of the
Investment Bankers Association, also with success. At these meetings, the
bankers agreed to a quota system among the major banking cities in the
country. New York was to raise $75,000 each year, Chicago $10,000, and
Philidelphia $6,000. No single banking house was to contribute more
than $5,000 in order to avoid "prejudice and criticism."[12]

Certain that this system would function nicely, the organizers reported
to the State Department on December 7 that they felt that they had a
solution. They prepared their final report and called a meeting of the
council for December 18, 1933, in Washington.[13] By that time, the
department had a box full of applications for jobs on the council's staff,
among them one from Fred Lavis, who had hoped to become identified
with the central protective agency proposed under Title II (chapter 3).[14]
Lavis had collected nine hundred signatures on a petition to create the
Title II corporation under the name of his Latin American Bondholders
Association, which he now admitted was defunct. He had then tried to get
the State Department to use LABA (really just Lavis) as the nucleus for the
private group rumored in the press. When that failed, Lavis hoped to be
involved in the FBPC, offering his services to Stevens. Max Winkler, for
his part, simply began a vigorous campaign against the FBPC, claiming
that it was a pawn of the issue houses, an ironic charge considering his
own backing.[15]

On the appointed day in December, the group that had met in October
convened again in the Treasury Building to hear the organizing committee
recommend that they incorporate themselves as the Foreign Bondholders
Protective Council, Incorporated. They had already filed papers of incorporation as a nonstock, nonprofit organization under the laws of Mary-
land that morning.[16] All eighteen of those invited to the October conference and Pierre Jay, a member of one of the original organizing efforts,
became the first directors. The group elected Stevens as president, Bell and
Dartmouth President Ernest Hopkins as vice presidents, and an executive
committee of seven with the addition of Jay, Thacher, Traphagen, and
Chubb.[17] It was damp and dismal outside the windows of the old
Treasury Building that day in December of 1933, but inside the sun of
optimism shown brightly.[18]

Basically, the council's charter charged it with the protection of the holders of obligations of foreign governments, whether governmentally guaranteed or direct loans, by the negotiation of debt settlements. The council could solicit the deposit of bonds, but would probably not do so. It would also collect and publish statistics and information concerning foreign bonds. Essentially, the Foreign Bondholders Protective Council would closely parallel the British Council of Foreign Bondholders, but it would not be as closely tied to the national government. It would have three types of members. "Full members" would be the directors, who would pay no dues and have the power to vote. Paying dues, but without vote, would be "contributing members," who would gain membership by a periodic monetary donation to the council. "Founders" would pay a fixed sum for a lifetime membership.[19] The nineteen directors would be elected to staggered three-year terms, and only the president, a staff, and counsel (Clark) would receive remuneration other than travel and that for services rendered.[20]

The optimistic organizers believed that they could easily solve the finance problem. They estimated a yearly expense of $100,000 for such items as salaries and travel, to come in from those most likely to benefit from the successes of the council: financial institutions under the city quota system, issue houses, manufacturers, banks, others engaged in the import-export business, and, finally, the foundations. They foresaw no machinery to collect these funds other than via the quota system and the membership program.[21] In this time of public and institutional impecuniosity, such a view marked the council's founders as short-sighted and perhaps a bit naive. As it turned out, the only people with a combination of enough money and interest to contribute were the financial institutions, who were not supposed to be involved.

Immediately following the council meeting of December 18, Stevens left for New Hampshire for a "vacation." Extremely ill, he turned the critical initial work of the council over to Chubb, Jay, Thacher, and Traphagen in New York. The remainder of the directors returned to their home areas to drum up both moral and financial support for the group. The four New York functionaries set up temporary offices for the FBPC in the Bank of New York and Trust Company Building at 48 Wall Street. By the end of the year, the optimism with which the council had begun seemed to be vindicating itself. Contributions, mostly from banks and houses of issue, started flowing. The politicians, the press, and foreign governments were making comments that augured well for the council's success. Many tied the council's efforts closely to the chances for a revival of foreign trade. All of this elicited nearly audible sighs of relief from the White House and the State Department.[22]

In the meantime, having completed his mission at Montevideo, Clark found himself deep in negotiation on the Niemeyer plan with the Brazilian minister of finance, Dr. Oswaldo Aranha, after a short delay because of a political shake-up in Brazil. Clark's mission was particularly critical to the council for two reasons: First, and obviously, it was the council's first effort, and hence the tenor of the Brazilian negotiations would undoubtedly set the tone for future FBPC endeavors. Second, the Niemeyer plan had elements that would not serve the American bondholders' cause well.[23] If Brazil issued a decree on debt readjustment based on that plan, without any revision, other debtor states would probably follow suit, and the council would have to combat the same unsatisfactory elements in each decree.

During January 1934, Clark argued with Aranha over six points of the Niemeyer plan discriminatory against dollar bonds. Remarkably, the persistent Clark managed to secure acceptance of the council's position to some degree on all six points, and as the negotiations ended, only a few minor objections to the Brazilian decree remained. The most important stipulated that "the option held by certain bondholders to demand payment in alternative currency at a fixed rate of charge, be temporarily withdrawn."[24] Under this method of overcoming the foreign exchange problem, the obligor nation could pay interest in its own inflated currency. Clark and Aranha finished their discussions by the end of January, and the Brazilian government issued its final decree on February 5, 1934.[25]

As Clark was finishing his stay in Rio, Chubb, Jay, Thacher, and Traphagen met daily in New York. Stevens's condition had not improved, and the four were devoting almost full time to the flood of work coming upon the council. The State Department had discharged the problem of defaulted bonds completely, and hundreds of letters concerning the default situation arrived daily at 48 Wall Street. Also time-consuming were the financial problem (the system of collection needed much perfecting) and the German debt situation. John Foster Dulles had gone to Berlin during the summer of 1933 to negotiate with the defaulting German government. Having achieved nothing, he returned to Germany in January 1934, this time with the sanction and cooperation of the council. Shortly afterward, the council dispatched Laird Bell to Berlin to join

Dulles. The Germans were threatening to reduce the service on their external bonds to an effective zero.[26] To make matters worse, defaults continued to grow in number, as did the proliferation of independent committees. Clark's Brazilian success notwithstanding, a pall of crisis settled over the council in its second month of operation due primarily to Stevens's continued absence. It was increasingly difficult for the New York members to do justice to the council while trying to service their regular responsibilities.[27]

As a counterpoise to all this confusion in New York, Clark stopped in the Dominican Republic, where he persuaded President Rafael Trujillo to open negotiations with the council on the reamortization of the Dominican external debt, now largely in default. With this icing on his cake, the triumphant lawyer continued on to New York, arriving on February 15. He exuded great confidence to the press concerning the future of the council. Certain that his successes would prompt other governments to approach the council for similar negotiations, Clark predicted that the council would soon solve the whole foreign securities problem. His thumping successes in Brazil and Santo Domingo were proof, he said, of the great potential within the FBPC "to treat with foreign governments more successfully than private committees organized to look out for one particular issue only."[28]

Before Clark's return, the four New Yorkers who carried the bulk of the council's workload decided that the Stevens situation had created an intolerable burden upon them. After moving the council offices out of Traphagen's bank and across the block to 90 Broad Street, they decided that the council needed an active president who could devote full time to the growing body of work before the organization. Reuben Clark's notable flourishes on behalf of the council in Latin America made him the natural candidate to take up the mantle. Consequently, a few days after Clark arrived in New York, the executive committee met in special session and elected him acting president while granting Stevens an indefinite leave of absence. Clark agreed to take the position only on a temporary basis, stipulating that he could not serve for more than six months.[29] Two months later, he would assume the permanent presidency of the Foreign Bondholders Protective Council, this time on the condition that he serve only until September 1, 1934.[30]

These stipulations for such temporary service raise three pertinent questions: Why was Clark so reluctant to commit himself to longer periods of service? And if so reluctant, why did he agree to serve at all?

Why was the council so willing and anxious to have him as president on such a provisional basis? As for the first, since April 6, 1933, Clark had been a member of the First Presidency of the Mormon church (officially the Church of Jesus Christ of Latter-day Saints). Within the Mormon ecclesiastical system, there is no professional clergy. Hence, in his position as second counselor to Mormon President Heber J. Grant (who had been in the insurance business), Clark was third in the spiritual and temporal hierarchy of the church. The Saints regard this ruling troika as the latter-day successor to that of Jesus's three chief apostles, Peter, James, and John.[31] For this reason, Clark could not commit himself for a long period of service in New York as a full-time council officer. Indeed, it is surprising that he would accept at all. But Reuben Clark believed that service to his country was the ultimate loyalty: "It is not enough that you be loyal in the passive sense in all these things; you must be actively loyal; and active loyalty is service, loyal to your government, the greatest gift you can bestow upon it."[32] And in his moralistic heart, there was more at stake than a few million dollars in bonds. "Unofficially," wrote his biographer Frank W. Fox, "as Reuben seemed to believe, the council was charged with preserving the canons of responsibility which underlay modern society."[33] Clark accordingly agreed to serve temporarily and to take a cut in salary (from $20,000 to $15,000) so that he could devote some time to his church duties at Mormon headquarters in Salt Lake City.[34]

Answers to the final question do not emerge so readily. Clark's qualifications for the position were substantial, although he admitted some ignorance of international finance. "For my part, I am not a financier, and I am not a banker (some say there is a distinction between them)," he told the Investment Bankers Association. "I never bought a bond, I never owned a bond, and, I regret to say, I was never a member of one of these preferential lists for underwriting securities. So what I do not know about bonds is all that you gentlemen do know."[35] As a diplomat, Clark could claim some considerable expertise. During his long record of service within the State Department (on and off and in various positions since 1906) he had often demonstrated an uncanny ability to obtain his goals with great force but without offense. This demeanor, combined with his stocky physique, elicited the following appraisal from Herbert Feis: "The most stubborn and acquisitive of all was J. Reuben Clark, Jr., . . . a really hard-fisted Mormon."[36] In addition, his apparent availability made him particularly attractive. It seemed to his non-Mormon colleagues on the council that Clark was virtually unemployed.

Also decisive was Clark's string of successes at international negotiations. Before his recent work in Montevideo, Rio, and Santo Domingo, he had served on several arbitration committees over the years, and his terms as assistant to Dwight Morrow and then as ambassador in Mexico City during the Hoover administration were fraught with intense negotiations, particularly over the oil question.[37] Clark's expositions on the orderly arbitration of international disputes had become legal canons and fit precisely the premises upon the which the council based its hopes. "Under the existing conditions of the world," he had written in 1913, nations will not, "submit questions to determination of arbitral tribunals unless they have the confidence and assurance that the tribunal will in its deliberations and determinations be guided by the fixed and settled rules and principles properly applicable and controlling."[38] Philander Knox once called him "the most helpful man in international law in the United States."[39] Given its predilections, the council could do no better.

The Foreign Bondholders Protective Council promised a heavy workload, and its directors needed someone willing to take on the task. And J. Reuben Clark was the embodiment of the Protestant ethic. As he once quipped, "My first name is work, my middle name is work, and my last name is work."[40] True to the Max Weber model, labor for Clark was not merely an economic means; it was a spiritual end.[41] He epitomized the Mormon concept of a strenuous and exacting life that leads to the fulfillment of a calling.[42] In Mormon doctrine, people are "foreordained" or endowed before birth with certain possibilities and capabilities. It is then up to each individual to strive upward through hard work in order to reach the full stature of that preexistent calling. Indeed, the enthronement of "honest labor" is in itself a part of Mormon doctrine. "Thou shalt not be idle," wrote Mormon founder Joseph Smith in 1831, "for he that is idle shall not eat the bread nor wear the garments of the laborer."[43] To this, Clark added, "You cannot be successful at anything and waste your time. And when I say work, I mean work. You who want to work forty hours a week and that is all, go to it. You will begin your life there and that is where you will end it. You have got to work more than that if you are going to get anywhere in this world."[44]

In classic Weberian fashion, Clark also believed in the rational enterprise of law,[45] and foremost in this structure of natural law was the right to own and to preserve the fruit of labor, private property:

> Men must return to the faith that to all mankind, not to some only, was the original decree. "Man shall eat bread by the sweat of

his brow," which means that if he would eat he must work. We who work owe to no well man a life in idleness. We must have the faith that that which a man rightfully gets by honest toil is his, and that no man and no power may rightfully take it from him without just compensation; that no man must be compelled against his will to work for another; and that no man may be forcefully kept from honest work which he is able, willing, and wishes to do.[46]

In short, Clark's philosophy fit him splendidly for the job of going after the defaulted foreign bonds. He could be nothing else than "stubborn and acquisitive." For what a man earned was his. The foreign debts were to be paid. There could be no other answer, even if the bonds were supposed to be as dead as Ezekiel's dry bones.

After assuming the leadership of the council, Clark characteristically submerged himself in the work. He announced plans for a vigorous campaign to expand the membership base to banks all over the country, to producers and manufacturers, and even chambers of commerce. He also declared that the council would become a permanent fixture in the American financial structure to prevent the occurrence of another such unfortunate foreign securities situation. The council, said Clark, would take upon itself the responsibility of overseeing in a "disinterested and independent" way the creditor position of the United States. After this flurry of activity, Reuben Clark sat down to dinner at the University Club on Monday, February 26, 1934, with Laird Bell, who had just returned from Berlin, and Tom Thacher. As Clark drank his customary teetotaling five or six glasses of water with the meal, he foretold the prophesying to come. The bones would live again.[47]

CHAPTER

5

A Really Hard-fisted Mormon

Thus saith the Lord God unto these bones;
Behold, I will cause breath to enter into you,
and ye shall live:

By the end of February 1934, the Roosevelt administration had reason
to wonder what had happened to its plans for dealing with the defaulted
foreign securities. New Deal officials had counted upon the services of
Ray Stevens, with whom they had carefully collaborated on the establishment of the sensitive Foreign Bondholders Protective Council. Roosevelt
at first had many doubts about the project, but his choice of Stevens had
worked out well, and his apprehensions eased.[1] Now, Reuben Clark had
assumed Stevens's position, and the administration was forced to undergo
a complete reevaluation of expected performance. They knew Clark well
enough, but they had not counted upon anyone but Stevens, whose
absence the president continued to believe was only temporary.[2] But
Clark's presidency came as a worrisome surprise. A stalwart of the ancien
regime, the Utah lawyer had been a long-time key functionary of Republican diplomacy, hardly a qualification to set him well with New Dealers.[3]
And all those frustrated holders of defaulted foreign bonds must have
wondered into whose hands their fate had fallen. Had the mountain
brought forth a mouse or a magician?

The story of J. Reuben Clark began after the Civil War, when his father,
a young veteran from Indiana, went west to be a miner, first in Montana,
then in Tooele County, Utah Territory. He became a Mormon, married
the daughter of a prominent Mormon bishop, and settled down to raise a

family and some cattle. The family's small stone house was where the first Clark child, his father's namesake, was born on September 1, 1871. Nine more children would follow. The environment in which young Reuben reached manhood was austere. The Great Salt Lake desert yielded grudgingly a meager living, and the boy had to shoulder very early a great deal of responsibility. He spent countless hours riding and caring for his father's small band of horses, but he also took an early interest in education. He learned to read and to write before he entered school at the age of ten in his hometown of Grantsville, Utah.[4]

His thirst for education unsatisfied after eight grades in a one-room school, Clark entered the Latter-day Saints College in Salt Lake City at the age of nineteen. At the college, he came under the influential tutelage of James E. Talmage, a renowned Mormon scholar and theologian who was then president of the institution. Talmage, later a Mormon apostle, was a geologist who subscribed largely to the social doctrines of Herbert Spencer.[5] He took Clark in hand and encouraged his industriousness and seriousness, appointing him clerk of the Deseret Museum, of which Talmage served as curator. In the meantime, the senior Clark had embarked upon an unsubsidized proselytizing mission for the church in the Midwest. Young Reuben went to work full-time for Talmage in order to support his father and family, "working ten hours a day and six days a week for fifty dollars a month."[6] In September 1894, Clark became secretary to Talmage and enrolled at the University of Utah, where Talmage had become president. Three years later, Clark emerged with an enhanced work ethic, a bachelor of science degree, and as valedictorian of his class.[7]

Shortly after graduation, Clark married Luacine Savage in the Salt Lake Temple and began a career in education. After teaching Latin, English, typing, shorthand, and civics and serving in various administrative positions for nearly five years, he became dissatisfied with his adequacy as a teacher.[8] This, no doubt, had much to do with his decision to enter law school at Columbia University in the fall of 1903. In New York, Clark quickly gained recognition for outstanding ability and effort, becoming editor of the *Columbia Law Review* and attracting the high praise of his mentors. One of these, George D. Parkinson, later wrote an article about Clark's remarkable abilities for a Mormon church magazine.[9] More significantly, James Brown Scott, another professor, hired him as an assistant to aid in the preparation of briefs.[10]

Before Clark's graduation from Columbia, he was admitted to the New York Bar. In the meantime, Scott had become solicitor for the

Department of State—technically, an assistant attorney general in the Justice Department—and rendered legal opinions on the work of the State Department. Scott brought the new lawyer with him to Washington, where Secretary of State Elihu Root had Clark appointed an assistant solicitor on September 5, 1906. As if those duties were not enough, Clark also taught at George Washington University as assistant professor of law while working for Scott at Foggy Bottom.[11] Among those in Washington whom Clark impressed immediately was Philander Knox, then attorney general. "I am doing [Clark] but justice," said Knox, "in saying that for natural ability, integrity, loyalty, and industry, I have not, in a long professional and public experience, met his superior and rarely his equal."[12] Consequently, when Knox became secretary of state under President William Howard Taft in 1909, he appointed Clark acting solicitor and later solicitor.[13] While in the Solicitor's Office, Clark wrote a monograph on citizenship for the Bureau of Naturalization,[14] worked on Russian extradition cases,[15] and managed to gain some $2.3 million in awards for American citizens before various international claims tribunals.[16] He also helped to draft numerous treaties and wrote an influential memorandum justifying armed intervention by executive order to protect American life and property abroad. The department considered this policy guide a classic authority on intervention and used it extensively for two decades.[17] With lifetime membership in the American Society of International Law, Clark had turned his career permanantly to international law.

In 1912, Clark became a director of the American Peace Society and was elected a member of the American Society for Judicial Settlement of International Disputes. These two concepts—the outlawry of war and the peaceful resolution of international disputes through judicial arbitration—were to remain among the central passions of his life.[18] Largely because of his interest in these other areas and due to the changing of the guard in Washington in 1913, he left the State Department[19] to become general counsel for the United States before the British-American Claims Commission, where he worked with Dwight Morrow of New Jersey.[20] Following this service, Clark practiced law in Washington until the American entry into World War I in 1917. He then took a commission in the Judge Advocate General Corps, the legal branch of the army, and became adjutant to the provost marshall general.[21] Stationed in Washington, and with the rank of major, Clark had the duty of analyzing war legislation passed in Congress and worked largely in the offices of

Attorney General Thomas Watt Gregory.[22] After Clark's discharge in December 1918, General Enoch H. Crowder recommended to Congress he be awarded the Distinguished Service Medal (which he received in 1922).[23]

With the end of the war, Clark made a detailed analysis of the Treaty of Versailles at the request of the State Department.[24] During the course of this effort, his opposition to the League of Nations concept grew increasingly vehement, and a third great passion of his life surfaced—isolationism. "It would be difficult for me to find language which would sufficiently express my abhorrence [for] this alliance idea" wrote Clark. "I am unalterably opposed to the League."[25] While his findings did not please Wilson's State Department, they attracted considerable attention among the anti-league clique in the Senate. Among these "irreconcilables" was Philander Knox, now senator from Pennsylvania, who invited Clark to serve at his elbow as special adviser during the senatorial debates on American participation in the league. In that capacity, Clark read Knox's speeches before delivery, gave some addresses himself, and presented his typically careful opinions to the irreconcilables.[26]

Clark returned briefly to the private practice he had maintained in Washington, New York, and Salt Lake City, serving as counsel for international affairs to several interests. Among his clients were several firms active in the foreign bond market, such as American International Corporation and J. P. Morgan & Co.[27] Knox's enthusiasm over Clark's abilities, however, presaged the Utahn's quick return to public service when the Republicans regained control of the White House in 1921.[28] Consequently, he served as special counsel to the American delegation at the Washington Conference on the Limitation of Armaments and as assistant to Secretary of State Charles Evans Hughes at the conference. Between 1922 and 1926, he served intermittently on the British-American Claims Commission, and in 1926 became agent of the United States before the United States–Mexico General Claims Commission.[29] This brought him into contact once again with Dwight Morrow, who was now ambassador to Mexico. In 1927, while Clark worked in Washington filling in for Undersecretary of State Robert Olds (who had taken leave), Morrow asked Clark to become his legal adviser in Mexico City. Accordingly, Reuben moved his family to Mexico that fall, where he assisted Morrow in obtaining the favorable oil settlement of 1928.[30]

On July 7, 1928, Clark left Morrow's side and returned to Salt Lake City to seek the Republican nomination to the United States Senate. The day after his defeat at the state nominating convention in August, he received his commission as undersecretary of state from Secretary Frank B. Kellogg.[31] The position had been vacant for some time since Olds's departure to "make money."[32] Kellogg had offered Clark the job earlier and had held it open for him pending the outcome of Clark's try for the Senate.[33] Clark assumed his new post on August 31, 1928, the day before his fifty-seventh birthday. He served for less than a year, retiring on June 19, 1929.[34] Observers at the time interpreted his nomination to the second post in the State Department as a move on President Coolidge's part to cement relations between the United States and Mexico. For this reason, his appointment brought considerable praise on both sides of the border; the public would applaud any step that portended an easing of the tiresome tensions over Mexican–American relations.[35] Kellogg's appointment of Clark had other implications as well. The secretary was in the midst of his battle to get the Peace Pact of 1928 ratified, and he certainly knew that Clark's expertise in law and proven persuasive ability would aid greatly in that fight.[36]

Kellogg had decided before August 1928 that a redefinition of the much-abused but hallowed dogma of American foreign policy, the Monroe Doctrine, would have to come forth if the Peace Pact was to surmount objections that it would undermine the famous principles of 1823.[37] Clark's background of twenty years in close contact with inter-American affairs and the problem of intervention made him a logical choice for directing such a delicate operation as a new interpretation of the Monroe Doctrine. In any case, Clark tendered his resignation as undersecretary only weeks after the ratification of the pact on January 15, 1929. He would have left in March had not President Hoover prevailed upon him to remain until a replacement could be appointed. If for no other reason, Clark's assignment to the department rested upon the hope that he could succeed in satisfying the Senate with a definition of Monroe's pronouncement that would not threaten the pact.[38]

Almost immediately after Clark's arrival in Washington, Kellogg gave to the new undersecretary the job of reassessing the meaning of the Monroe Doctrine.[39] Clark in turn assigned his assistant Anna O'Neill the task of preparing a careful running summary of everything salient that had been said or done in the name of the doctrine. To this 238-page document Clark attached a seventeen-page cover letter which, by a strange quirk of fate, earned for him perhaps more mention in the history books than was accorded to any other undersecretary. With its seeming repudiation of the Roosevelt corollary of interventionism, Clark's *Memo-*

randum on the Monroe Doctrine[40] became a landmark in the historiography of United States–Latin American relations because it appeared to be a pivotal state paper, diverting American policy toward the "good neighbor" ideal. More recent scholarly examinations of the Clark Memorandum episode, however, have demonstrated that the document was really very conservative, merely rejustifying intervention under the more potent maxims of the right to self-defense. The government never accepted or used its contents as any part of its policy formulation, and the memorandum had nothing whatsoever to do with the Good Neighbor policy of Herbert Hoover and Franklin Roosevelt.[41]

The rest of Clark's brief term as undersecretary ran a comparatively insignificant course.[42] After spending much of his time filling in for Kellogg and his successor Henry Stimson, he left Washington in June of 1929, professing the intention of resuming his private practice in Utah.[43] Nevertheless, he soon returned to Mexico City and his former capacity as special advisor to Morrow.[44] It had become apparent that the ambassador would soon leave his successful mission. The most common rumor (prior to Stimson's appointment) declared that Hoover wanted Morrow to become secretary of state.[45] When that failed to happen, word spread that he was bound for the Senate. In any case, Clark's presence, along with that of other long-time Morrow aides, would shore up the ambassador's accomplishments and smooth the way for his departure.[46]

Because Morrow had left for Europe to attend the London Naval Conference, Hoover designated Clark in January 1930 as special ambassador to the February 5 inauguraton of Pascual Ortiz Rubio as president of Mexico. Clark took a conspicuous part in the inauguration pageantry, occupying the diplomatic box nearest the presidential stand. This signified not only the tremendous progress toward cordial relations that Morrow's tenure had generated, but also the acceptance of the familiar Clark in the Mexican capital.[47] But despite this obvious preparation of Clark as successor, when Morrow did announce his intention to become the new senator from New Jersey, rumors centered on George Rublee (another Morrow adviser and a former Woodrow Wilson aide) as the new envoy to Mexico.[48] Clark nevertheless received his appointment to the $17,500 per year position on October 3, 1930.[49] He left at once for Washington for a series of briefings at the State Department, but did not arrive back in Mexico City until November 11, 1930, because of Senator Reed Smoot's urgent appeal for him to participate in the Utah Republican campaign.[50]

General acclamation greeted the Clark nomination in official Mexican circles, where it appeared as a Hoover move to assure the continued conciliatory policies of the Dwight Morrow era. The Mexicans emphasized Clark's role in settling the oil dispute, and in general praised his personality. "Few are made like Clark," one high official said. "He was the man indicated for the job."[51] The correspondent of the *New York Times* added that Clark seemed acceptable to all factions in Mexico, and that many Mexicans were surprised that he had accepted because he was not wealthy like Morrow and could earn more in private practice.[52] There had been some amazement that the Wall Street "imperialist" Morrow had been able to win the Mexican confidence and respect. Although of clearly humbler circumstances, Clark also had the "Wall Street" label.[53]

American comment upon the nomination generally emphasized Clark's similarity to Morrow and the obvious hope for continuity of successful dealings with Mexico. It maintained that there could be no doubt that Clark was the best man for the job considering his training and role as understudy to Morrow.[54] A lengthy editorial in the *New York Times* gave much credit for Morrow's success to this "right-hand man" and "upholder of the Book of Mormon." It also noted that Clark's appointment was merely a formalization of the actual position he had held since January when his predecessor had gone to London. In words that might encourage the bondholders a few years later, the editorialist praised Clark as being adept at "studying the documents." He "knows the State Department, . . . what it wants, how it gets it and how its quaint but highly polished machinery works." Although there were many "experts" on Mexico who in actuality knew little about the country, Clark was "not that kind of expert. Together with Mr. Morrow he holds the working hypothesis about Mexican relations—that the other fellow is just as proud of his country as you are of yours. This ruddy-faced Mormon knows Mexico as well as he knows the State Department." The editorial's tone was jovial and full of confidence for Clark's chances of success, even though he was "to be the successor of conspicuous success." The writer could not resist poking fun at Clark's eating habits: "If Mr. Clark has any outstanding peculiarity, it is dietary. Breakfast means nothing to him. Luncheon is his first meal. Between meals he drinks fifteen or twenty glasses of water and a number of beakers of milk."[55]

On November 28, 1930, Clark presented his credentials to Ortiz Rubio in a private ceremony at the National Palace.[56] All indications were that his term would be full of cordiality and friendship between two countries that had nearly gone to war just three years before. As it developed, his service attracted so little notice that most historians of United States–Latin American relations mention his name only in connection with the overplayed Clark Memorandum. For the first time since the Revolution of 1910, news of Mexico and the doings of the American ambassador were not exciting, front-page news full of diplomatic brinksmanship.[57]

The trouble between the neighbors was not over, however, as Clark's successor, Josephus Daniels, quickly learned. There are two apparent reasons for the quietude of Clark's term between the two noisy eras of Morrow and Daniels. First, Ortiz Rubio and his provisional successor were conservatives under the thumb of the caudillo, Plutarco Calles. The old general had mellowed his "revolutionary" nature, and Clark was on friendly terms with the jefe. Second, Clark had come in on the heels of Dwight Morrow, unmistakably the conciliator of the age. Passions were cool. In addition, Clark always hoped to avoid noisy clashes of interest. He believed in keeping the lid on potential trouble by effecting careful negotiation before a situation could get out of hand. He gained the confidence and respect of the embassy personnel,[58] and stuck to Morrow's system of policies.[59] Like Morrow, Clark spent long hours devising means to protect American economic and strategic interests in a nation undergoing social revolution.[60] His peacemaker's personality, which observers characterized as "breezy" and "inconspicuous," satisfied all contenders and precluded harsh exchanges.[61] The most important achievement of Clark's three years in the embassy lay once again in his favorite field of claims. In a lump sum, or en bloc, agreement, he managed to scale down the American claim from an original 382 million pesos to an acceptable 10 million.[62]

Despite rumors that Roosevelt would reappoint him, Clark officially resigned his post in March 1933 to fill a vacancy in the First Presidency, the ruling triumvirate of the LDS Church.[63] In a Mormon conference on April 6, 1933, he assumed this ecclesiastical post to which he would devote the rest of his life. At that meeting in the Salt Lake Tabernacle, Clark acceded to what Mormons consider to be a position of "prophet, seer, and revelator" and preached a sermon on the "joy of work." If they had heard it along with the Mormon faithful, the people who held foreign bonds would also have found much inspiration in his address that day: "And save in extremity, no man may rightfully violate that law by living by the sweat from the brow of his brother." Inescapable and eternal law, thundered the new prophet, demands a "return to old-time virtues—

industry, thrift, honesty, self-reliance, independence of spirit, self-discipline, and mutual helpfulness."[64] Almost as if he would then prove the sincerity of such a clarion pronouncement, he would spend a great deal of time over the next few years fighting for an immutable virtue that could summarize them all, the payment of honest debts.

Had they made a similar survey of the new council's leader, State Department officials in February 1934 would thus have found a man with deep experience in foreign relations. Reuben Clark believed fervently in peace, in the resort to judicial means in international disputes, and in America's going it alone. Longing for a return to the old simplicity of things, he was a part of the great interwar isolationist impulse. He was also a nineteenth-century man from a frontier in the old universe who just happened to believe that he was literally a prophet after the order of Elijah, Jeremiah, and Ezekiel. He would preach the orthodox dogma against the withering onslaught of heretical notions from the false prophets of the New Deal.[65] His mission into the valley of defaulted foreign bonds fit nicely into his vision of who he was and to what service the Lord had called him. At the following October conference of the church, Clark spoke of his love for the United States: "I know my own mind and heart, next to God, the author of my being, comes my country. It has been my honor and my privilege to serve it in some more or less minor capacities, and if the providences of the Lord shall so order, I stand ready to serve again."[66] Those who held foreign bonds, to the occasional chagrin of the Roosevelt administration, had at the helm of their ship of hope a tenacious and uncompromising captain who believed in eternal law and traditional values, and that an honest debt is a sacred obligation.

6

Putting on the Mantle

And I will lay sinews upon you,
and will bring up flesh upon you,
and cover you with skin, and put breath in you,
and you shall live;
and ye shall know that I am the Lord.

The State Department was so eager to get the foreign bond situation off its hands that even before the official incorporation of the council on December 18, 1933, department officers answered all questions about the problem with copies of its October 20 press release about the pending organization. After December 18, they replied with a form letter. "The Department cannot undertake to advise you with respect to these bonds," it said. "The Foreign Bondholders Protective Council operates independently of the Government, and this reference is made wholly without responsibility on the part of the Department."[1] The department, nevertheless, remained naturally concerned about the council's image and power, anxious to distinguish between the council and that allowed under Title II of the Securities Act of 1933. The public showed an understandable inability to keep the ideas separate, because the Johnson plan had received so much publicity in the press before the formation of the FBPC.[2] The State Department also worried about whether the policies that seemed to be emerging during the first weeks of the body's operations would meet with its full approval. Cordell Hull, for example, had heard that the council would represent only those holding government or governmentally guaranteed bonds and not those who held foreign corporate bonds. "I fear this narrow policy will react seriously on interests of American citizens thus excluded from all aid. If report is true is there any way to consider expanding this proposed narrow policy?"[3] It was like the old problem of the mother who desired to see her child completely free and responsible, but who could not turn away from watching, hoping, and worrying.

Because of Stevens's illness and before Clark took the helm, a strong sense of trepidation existed in Washington over the newborn council's chances for success. But the New York members, on their own time, proved themselves devoted to the health of the infant effort. Through the month of January 1934, they carried forth a dedicated campaign to solicit funding and contributing members. They began auspiciously by persuading Henry L. Stimson to contribute the first $500 for a Founder's membership.[4] Subsequently, Andrew Mellon, Grenville Clark, Hendon Chubb, Alanson Houghton, Frank Lowden, and Thomas Thacher joined Stimson with large contributions.[5] The organizers then persuaded Allen Dulles to donate his services as counsel in the absence of Reuben Clark.[6] The New Yorkers had also instituted a widespread effort to obtain the support of bankers in New York, Chicago, Philadelphia, and Boston through the quota plan and with the help of the Federal Reserve structure.[7] The trouble was that they were attempting to accomplish a full-time job on a part-time basis. It was "a very unfortunate situation" in Jay's estimation, and they anticipated the arrival of Clark happily; they were even willing to accept his services on conditional terms.[8]

Clark assumed his office as acting president at a meeting of the executive committee on February 26. At that meeting, the group also appointed Allen Throop, another New York lawyer, as secretary of the committee, describing that job as "second in importance only to the Presidency."[9] It also increased its assessment of financial need to $150,000 and heard reports from Clark and Bell upon their recent negotiations in Brazil and Germany.[10] Other news included word that a bill making it illegal for a government in default to deal in securities in the United States had come to the floor of the Senate.[11]

The committee then turned its attention to a problem no one had anticipated—a rising tide of antagonistic comment in the press and elsewhere. Max Winkler seemed particularly unhappy with the FBPC, attacking it vigorously in whatever forum he could gain. In addition, several newspapers, Hearst's *New York American* in the forefront, were expanding greatly upon these criticisms in a campaign to discredit the new organization.[12] Most of the anti-council discussion at this point was groundless, and in Winkler's case at least, amounted only to sour grapes. Apparently, this tide of shallow criticism symbolized some sort of jealousy mingled with suspicion because the group claimed by its very nature to have the exclusive or preponderant right to deal with the lucrative business of resurrecting defaulted foreign securities. As time passed, this criticism, promising to be a nagging problem for the future of the FBPC, would grow and strengthen upon each of the council's inescapable errors or questionable policies.

After the February 26 meeting, Clark stayed in New York for a few days to meet with several interested parties to discuss the Brazilian arrangement. Mormon Church President Heber Grant then met him, and together they traveled to Salt Lake City, arriving on Tuesday morning, March 7. Clark had not seen his family in four months and was flirting with the notion of another try for the Senate, but he would stay only some four days before returning to New York and his new post, his new passion. He spent his time at home explaining the foreign bond situation to the Utah press corps and denying aspirations for the Senate seat of William King (although in reality he remained undecided). Then he and his wife entrained for New York on March 12.[12] Work, work always.

At 90 Broad Street for just two weeks this time, Clark familiarized himself with the work ahead and prepared for current and upcoming negotiations with Germany, Cuba, the Dominican Republic, and Colombia. An independent committee had seriously aggravated the Colombian situation,[14] bringing the need for complete council hegemony in the foreign default field into clear focus. Afraid of a similar embroglio in the pending Cuban negotiations, Clark sent letters to several institutions and asked their support for a council-sponsored Cuban committee "to forestall the creation of profit-making bondholders' committees."[15] His intentions were good, and perhaps even proper, but his request departed from the original plan to have the council merely coordinate and assist the independent groups. Sending a powerful signal that he would not tolerate interference in his province, Clark would bend every effort to centralize totally America's foreign bond negotiation endeavor.

By the time Clark left New York at the end of March for his church's annual conference,[16] he had become convinced that many defaulting countries "will soon be in a position where . . . a resumption of services, wholly or in part, will be possible."[17] He believed that many of the debtors were diverting dollars they were receiving through exports to the

United States to purposes other than debt payment.[18] Thus a hard-line philosophy appeared to develop in Clark's zeal to collect; he would draw the line between necessity and luxury over the expenditure of debtor revenue far into what the obligors would usually regard as the necessity side of the fiscal spectrum. He would go after the "ability to pay" aspect in his work with the debtor governments. He would easily earn Feis's "stubborn and acquisitive" sobriquet.[19] A debt was a supreme obligation. Only veritable survival should stand in the way of its satisfaction.

While Clark was in Utah in April, the Cuban foreign bond situation worsened substantially. The Cuban government had defaulted in December on its external public works bonds, and on April 10, 1934, it issued a decree suspending the amortization on two more large American loans (issued from the Speyer and Morgan houses) on the basis of "inability to pay."[20] On the sixteenth, the revolutionary government of Fulgencio Batista appointed a commission to investigate the loans the deposed dictator, Gerardo Machado, had obtained in the United States. No one doubted at the outset that the commission would conclude that the loans were illegal and therefore not binding upon the present government.[21] George Rublee, the council's unofficial intermediary in Washington, relayed the Cuban development to 90 Broad Street.[22] In addition, the Uruguayans had approached the council about the possibility of beginning negotiations over their defaulted issues.[23]

The executive committee met and decided first that Clark must assume the permanent presidency. Stevens would soon offer his resignation, and exigencies required the firm organization of the office. Clark agreed when he returned to New York, and inquiries about his acceptability went out to the directors.[24] Accordingly, Stevens resigned on April 24, and on May 8, Clark became the official president of the FBPC. However he retained the understanding that he could serve only until August 31; the executive committee believed that the change in title, if not in actual situation, would lend greatly to Clark's authority and hence ability to act forcefully in the accelerating circumstances.[25]

While all of this transpired in New York, Clark had turned his mind to another of his life's great causes, insulating the United States against the League of Nations concept. He traveled to Washington, where Senator Key Pittman's Committee on Foreign Relations was considering the advisability of the accession of the United States to the Permanent Court of International Justice, something Clark believed he had helped to bury a decade before. As he later argued, any connection with the league would signal a further abdication of American morality.

> In essence, the League of Nations is, by intention and by actual operation, a military alliance among the great powers of Western Europe, which, with their possessions and dominions and the flattered weak and small powers of the world, have regrouped themselves in a new balance of power arrangement. The real purpose of this alliance is to make secure to themselves the world-wide territorial, strategic, political, economic, and financial gains with which, through the intervention of the United States, they were able to enrich themselves at the end of the great war.[26]

Clark believed instead in "a world organization for the purposes of deliberation, but not for the purposes of waging wars and imposing sanctions. We must bring to bear in the solution of matters of world concern, that moral force of the world of which President Wilson rightly thought so highly."[27] Three years later, during a visit to league headquarters in Geneva, Clark would discuss the possibility of international machinery "to control future loans and prevent States from making loans when they were already practically insolvent."[28] But such world cooperation would have to wait, inasmuch as a great burden of preliminary obstacles remained. Aside from its attachment to the league, for example, his specific objections to the Permanent Court revolved around its failure to provide for a full codification of existing international law. "No nation may safely submit its conduct to compulsory review when it does not know first what it ought to do or is expected to do under given circumstances, and second by what rule its conduct under such circumstances will be judged. Thus a full codification of existing international law is indispensible to the creation of any wise and effective international judicial system with powers of compulsory jurisdiction."[29]

So on May 16, 1934, the foreign bond demands could wait while Clark joined George Pepper of Pennsylvania and James Reed of Missouri in testimony against the court before Pittman's committee. Clark held that the United States could not avoid becoming a de facto member of the league if it adhered to court protocol, because its power sprang from the covenant. And for Reuben Clark, that was reason enough to avoid all American connection with the concept.[30]

When Clark returned to New York from his isolationist mission to

Capitol Hill, he found that in addition to the Cuban situation, Germany appeared ready to issue a decree that promised to amend its discriminatory January proposal on its defaults. Bell and Jay had been in Berlin working with Reichsbank President Hjalman Schacht. Jay had just returned, and the council awaited anxiously the form of the new German statement. Schacht's intransigence had appalled Clark and the executive committee, but Jay's report was hopeful. On May 29, 1934, the Germans announced that they would either pay 40 percent of maturing coupons in cash, or replace them with a 3 percent funding bond for the full amount. In either case, the Germans were simply converting one class of default into another.[31] Clark, obviously disappointed, admitted that the council was unable "to approve this offer as fair, just and equitable to the American holders of German dollar bonds." It was, however, "the best that the Conference could induce Germany to make."[32] The council hoped nevertheless that Schacht would carry through with his January promise to continue interest payments through to July 1, and to register the scrip under the provisions of the Securities Act.[33]

With the German disappointment weighing heavily upon his mind, Clark journeyed west to receive an honorary degree at the University of Utah. Arriving in Salt Lake City on June 2, he addressed a greeting party at the station and lamented the German experience, but added that it was much better than no offer at all. After all, Schacht had said in 1933 that the United States would get nothing.[34] Clark believed the German discrimination against American holders resulted from the United States having a favorable balance of trade with the Germans, which meant that they were short on exchange and willing to let those nations with an unfavorable balance (such as Switzerland and the Netherlands) take off import costs for the service of the Berlin debt.[35] On a brighter side, he anticipated the beginnings of work with Uruguay, Colombia, Chile, Peru, and, hopefully, with some European states. "We are now trying to make these extreme ends meet on some common ground," he said. "The Council has already accomplished considerable and expects its service for the coming year to do even better things for the American holders of foreign bonds."[36]

Clark received his degree, took a short trip to Los Angeles to gain support for the council on the West Coast, looked over the political picture in Utah, and left for New York on June 12 aboard the Los Angeles Limited.[37] By June 18, 1934, he had decided, after a long silence, not to make another try for the Senate. He advised the Republican state chairman that he was not a candidate and asked his friends to discontinue their efforts on his behalf.[38] He gave no overt indication of his reasons. Certainly, the fact that political prognostications had pronounced the popular King's seat secure had a great deal to do with Clark's decision, as did opposition from the president of the church. Even though he had concocted a plan whereby he would meld his religious service with senatorial duties, Clark never felt entirely comfortable in doing so.[39] He was still talking of retirement from the FBPC presidency in the fall, but having decided against the Senate as a platform for civic activity, he may already have concluded to remain indefinitely in the forefront of the bondholders' fight. Elements in the council situation in June 1934 doubtlessly appealed to Clark's predilections. Two factors in particular might have induced him to persevere at 90 Broad Street—plenty of work and a growing criticism of the council. Clark enjoyed coming to grips with both.[40]

As for the first, when Clark arrived in New York, the Germans still had not registered their scrip. Bell had indicated the council's disappointment to Schacht but had received no reply.[41] Clark accordingly sent Schacht a polite but chiding telegram to remind him of his solemn promises. The Brooklyn-born German's answer was silence. In the meantime, as arrangements progressed to service German bonds held in other nations, discrimination against U.S. holders had not abated. Holding a favorable balance of trade with every creditor but the United States, Germany quickly entered into debt service agreements with those other states while leaving the dollar bonds in default.[42]

On this side of the Atlantic, the Cuban government commission, as expected, declared that bonds floated during the "illegal" Machado regime were null and void.[43] In the face of this gross repudiation, Clark pressed forward with his plans for a protective committee for those who held Cuban bonds.[44] And on June 29, President-elect Alfonso Lopez of Colombia arrived in New York to meet with Clark. Conferring with Lopez in the Colombian's suite at the Waldorf Astoria, Clark discussed the Colombian bond situation in detail, emphasizing the financial advantages to Colombia of "making provision for some proper and adequate service" on its dollar-bond obligations. Lopez assured Clark that he would "carefully investigate Colombia's entire financial situation" and keep the council advised.[45] An abundance of work was developing for the council and Reuben Clark.

In the second regard, Herbert Feis had received a serious complaint against Clark from one of the FBPC's directors. Believing that the president and the executive committee had too much authority at the expense of the directors, Quincy Wright, professor of international law at the University of Chicago, criticized Clark for cancelling meetings and for a general failure to include the directors in the policymaking process.[46] In light of this criticism, Clark decided to tighten the organization of the board of directors with the appointment of a chairman. He wanted to bring a former State Department colleague, Francis White, into this new and important slot on the council, but various administration officials immediately raised rather nonspecific objections to the move.[47] White had been an assistant secretary at State during the Coolidge and Hoover administrations. But as chairman of the Commission of Neutrals on the Chaco War, he had offended Europeans and many Latin Americans by openly discouraging the League of Nations from sending investigators to the scene of the fighting in Bolivia and Paraguay in 1932. Probably also damaging in the light of the Good Neighbor policy, White had made statements while assistant secretary that smacked of old American hegemonist notions under the Monroe Doctrine à la Theodore Roosevelt.[48]

Clark also learned at about this time through Rublee that FDR was unhappy with some of the council's actions and felt that Clark was not keeping him informed. Hoping to overcome this problem quickly, Clark wrote to Feis: "Do you suppose there is any way in which you could get some sort of a summary over to the President? A report from us direct would, of course, mean merely to have it referred over to you by some subordinate in the White House offices. Have you any suggestions to offer in this?"[49] Feis suggested that either the council send a condensed report, or that Clark come to Washington, where the State Department would try to get him in to see the president.[50] Wanting to discuss the White appointment with State anyway, Clark chose to visit the capital.

Upon his arrival, he called at the State Department on June 28, 1934, and attempted to arrange a meeting with Roosevelt. Realizing that a White House visit did not appear likely, he devoted his attentions to the White question. Evidently convinced by the extent of the opposition against his friend, he told Undersecretary William Phillips that he had come to the conclusion that it would be better to withdraw White's name. He also submitted three other names for consideration for the post, but failing to get White, he evidently dropped his plans for a board chairmanship.[51] Despite his failures to see Roosevelt and to get White approved, his visit nevertheless appears to have reaffirmed the department's support for the council. For example, department officers began to assert even more strongly than before its policy "that the settlement of such obligations is a matter for direct negotiation and agreement between the representatives of such bondholders and the debtor governments," and continued to refer all foreign bond questions to the council.[52] Clark had somehow managed to allay most of the administration's suspicions that had grown with the rising flow of criticism of the council in the press and mail.

In New York, Schacht's silence elicited another inquisitive cable from Clark, this one somewhat less polite.[53] Consequently, the Reichsbank assured the council that it was working on the registration problem,[54] but in the meantime, the Germans began to demonstrate discrimination against the Americans who held Dawes and Young bonds in their agreements for service with the British and Dutch. It seemed that Schacht was purposefully compounding his problems with American holders while pretending to want an acceptable solution. Clark appealed to his sense of justice:

> The original German promise to serve such bonds held by the nationals of other countries is the same promise Germany made to serve such bonds held by Americans. The credit of Germany is as much involved in serving bonds held by Americans as in serving bonds held by anyone else. To serve the Dawes and Young bonds held by the nationals of other countries and to decline to serve the bonds held by Americans would constitute the grossest discrimination and would be violative of every principle of justice and fair dealing.[55]

Again the Germans replied with silence.

On July 25, the directors of the council assembled to discuss the Germans' intransigence. Clark confined this long-overdue meeting to a luncheon at which he reported on the council's labors and outlined ways in which the directors would develop support for the work in their respective areas of the country. Despite Wright's criticism, it was apparent that Clark and the executive committee intended to continue to control the effort without any advice and consent from the board of directors. With humor and blithe deportment, Clark won their acquiescence. "By my talking to the Directors all the time they were eating and so spoiling a good lunch for them," Clark wrote Newton Baker, "we were able to get through at the close of the luncheon period."[56] There would be no more criticism from council members. The group also discussed the organization's relationship with the State Department and made something of a declaration of independence. "In any situation, the Council should consider the views of the Department of State as one of the factors determining its actions in any given case, but should not necessarily be controlled by such views."[57]

In the midst of the difficult German situation, the council received some extremely happy news in the Dominican Republic's case. Early in the summer, the negotiations that Clark had urged upon Trujillo were beginning to pay dividends, and on August 10, Trujillo offered to resume payments on two loans under full interest. The maturity date would be extended considerably, and on the part of the United States, a general receivership of customs and small amortization payments would go into effect. The offer was a culmination of discussions Clark and three of Trujillo's representatives had undertaken intermittently since March 26.[58] An exultant Clark studied the form of the Dominican offer, and replied: "The Council feels your proposal fair to the Republic and the Dominican people and consistent with the broad equities and long-view interests of the bondholders, being indeed in some respects distinctly advantageous to them over their present situation."[59] To this he added the council's

> grateful appreciation of the spirit of tolerance and accommodation which had characterized the discussions carried on by your representatives, and to express the Council's congratulations that in the midst of the world depression the Dominican Government, under your distinguished leadership, is willing to undertake to serve its public debt, not only by paying the full interest but also by making continuous the payment on account of amortization, so recognizing the necessity of meeting both elements of a public debt service.[60]

Clark would expect nothing less than the same from the other debtors.

The council recommended the Dominican offer to the Department of State, which subsequently accepted and acclaimed it.[61] In both the United States and Latin America, the plan elicited a shower of praise for the council and for the "Good Neighbor Policy of President Roosevelt and Secretary Hull which made this adjustment possible."[62] In financial circles, a chorus of voices hailed it as a great triumph for the council and an important step toward the adjustment of all defaulted foreign bonds in America.[63] Cynical brokers, who had thought the straight-laced Clark a laughable phony, began to realize that his hard-line moral stance on the issue might just pay off.[64] Basking in the new light of his accomplishment, Clark determined that this was an opportune time to spur other Latin Americans to begin negotiations. He would capitalize to the greatest extent upon the thumping Dominican success.[65]

No one seemed to notice in the face of all this positive activity that Clark's deadline for the end of his service was fast approaching. The Dominican effort climaxed the first year of the council, and as summer ended, Clark could be sure that the mantle had properly descended and that the prophesying was true. With a concomitant sense of great satisfaction, he left New York on August 23 for Utah, arriving three days later. The Dominican episode had made him a local hero; because of Clark, the people of Utah perhaps knew more about the foreign bond situation than those of any other state. The press was consequently anxious to learn of his FBPC plans; he would only say that they were "uncertain." As Clark settled down to his church duties, he gave no indication about whether he would return to New York and the leadership of the council.[66]

Within a few days, however, he headed east again, dedicated to launching a fall schedule full of writing and speech-making in support of the FBPC. He had written a lengthy article for *Current History Magazine*, however, the editors wanted to make drastic cuts in the piece. The thrust of the article, in addition to recounting the history of the council and the foreign bond problem, was "that the bond is the obligation of the government to be met by the government," and that the issue houses should stay out of discussions toward adjustment lest the bondholder "be made to suffer."[67] Designed to bolster the council's claim to exclusivity in negotiating with defaulting lenders, the article could bear no cuts as far as Clark was concerned and never came to print, although the editors offered every compromise.[68]

Speeches would give a greater degree of freedom, so Clark had accepted a calendar full of invitations for the next few months. Just before returning to Salt Lake City for the fall conference of the church, he addressed the Bond Club of Philadelphia, where he articulated reasons why the use of armed force or seizing revenues to secure payments was out of the question. Only the council's efforts could succeed, but they would need the unified backing of the financial community.[69]

At the October LDS conference, Clark was advanced to the position of first counselor in the church presidency, the number-two spot in the Mormon hierarchy.[70] In contrast to the support for the New Deal the church had professed just a year before, at this conference, several leaders launched frontal attacks upon federal relief programs. Clark's speech urged Mormons not to soil their hands "with the bounteous outpouring of funds" under the New Deal welfare system. "What we get, we members of the Church, compared with the total mass that is distributed, is almost microscopic, but the spirit in which we might take it, the spirit in which we might spend it, is the leaven that might leaven the whole lump."[71] He spoke for property and equated the fanatical plans for the redistribution of wealth abroad in the land as a "substitute for the law that has come to us for over thirty-five hundred years, 'Thou shalt not steal,' and 'Thou shalt not covet.' They would substitute the opposite: 'Steal from those who have. Covet all that your neighbor possesses.'"[72] For Clark, there could be no separation between the functionings of society and the order of religion. An assault upon Americanism was an assault upon such hallowed instruments as the Ten Commandments. To be patriotic, to be in favor of America (and the collection of American credits) was to be in favor of godliness and spiritual health.

During Clark's sojourn in Utah, and during the hiatus in FBPC activity, an interesting episode in his public life unfolded. An American oil lobbyist had approached Ambassador Josephus Daniels with a plan to invite Clark to Mexico City "to try to iron out current difficulties"[73] that had once again arisen over the nationalization of the Mexican oil industry. It seemed that perhaps Clark's old magic would work on the new man in the National Palace, Lazaro Cardenas. Daniels was understandably insulted, the State Department refused to become involved, and even Clark opposed the plan. The oil companies, nevertheless, offered to pay his expenses, and Clark reluctantly agreed to come. Arriving in Mexico in November 1934 in a completely unofficial capacity, Clark pulled all of the strings he knew, including those of the slipping strongman Calles. But he quickly learned, as would everyone else, that Cardenas was a new commodity in Mexican politics. The mission failed completely and remained an embarrassment to Clark—a sour final chapter in his otherwise pleasant memories of Mexico.[74]

In Clark's absence from New York and as the euphoria of the Dominican success wore off, the executive committee began to discover that two old and seemingly solved problems had worsened. First, the financial support base had begun to weaken, and the banks were becoming increasingly reluctant to commit themselves over a long haul to sustain the council.[75] The second problem was that the Department of State had resumed questioning the FBPC's ability, if left to its own course, to solve the default problem. The principal antagonist in the department, strangely enough, turned out to be Herbert Feis. Feeling what he later admitted to be a "personal grudge" against the officers of the council,[76] Feis told Hull that his faith in the council was wearing thin. He proposed a plan for new international machinery, maybe through the Financial Section of the League of Nations. Feis said that his main worry over the events of 1934 was that "the treatment of debts has become so intertwined with the bilateral trade relationships between different countries and so dependent on clearing and compensate agreements of a bilateral character, that the former community of interest among creditor groups of different countries has been pretty well destroyed."[77] Hull did not act on Feis's suggestion, but this problem, along with the organization's heavy dependence upon the banking houses for financial support, would prove to be heavy millstones about the council's neck during the next few years.

On the administrative side, the council solved the problem of Clark's presidency. He would remain as president, but in order that he might spend more time in Salt Lake City, an alter ego would accede to a new high position. In essence, the presidency would become a sort of dual office. In December, the council (at Clark's insistence) elected Francis White as executive vice president and secretary. White had already resigned his position as a vice president of International Telephone and Telegraph in anticipation of his new post.[78] He would receive a $15,000 salary, $10,000 as secretary, and $5,000 from Clark's compensation.[79] In a model compromise, Clark would remain, but at the same time, he would not.

And so ended the first year of the Foreign Bondholders Protective Council, and of Clark's service as its prophet. The experience of 1934 traced some important patterns for the future and was perhaps the most important period of the council's history. Some definite philosophies, policies, and methods of operation had emerged that would map the route for the council's future, and most of the problems that would chronically bedevil the organization had already arisen. The bondholders' effort, with Clark at its head, had taken on the responsibility, had put on the mantle. Clark became the council, imbuing it with his philosophies and sense of anachronistic morality. In 1934, the FBPC was Reuben Clark, a champion of the old universe. Wright's criticism that Clark ran the council without advice and consent may thus have been absolutely accurate.

Clark believed that the sacrifice required on the part of the debtors in a resumption of bond service (such as the diversion of revenue, additional taxation or the export of gold) ought to be pushed to the limit. He would use two levers primarily to obtain this sacrifice—restoring the good reputation of the debtor state and restituting a good credit rating. Even though he believed foreign lending to be a vice, and although subsequent history would render the credit-rating issue meaningless, he would use the latter ploy effectively.[80] Clark had become convinced that the only lasting solution to the foreign securities problems lay within expanding international trade.[81] Delivering a series of speeches that fall, he pleaded for continuing loans in order to finance activities that would enhance trade with borrowers, so that debtors in turn could use the revenues from that trade to service their obligations to American citizens, who were losing a great deal of money every day under the defaults.[82] While urging investment bankers to maintain their financial support until fees from defaulters and bondholders could support the council,[83] Clark left no question about whom the organization represented. "We are not always going to please all of you, and perhaps most of the time we will please none of you, but our intentions are good. We are trying to look after the interests of the bondholders."[84]

Finally, although enjoying its independence from the federal government, the council would carefully court the approval of the State Department and other agencies in Washington in order to maintain as completely as possible administration support and cooperation.[85] This would be a large and difficult problem, but the council would meet each threat to its power with the skillful diplomacy and persuasive humor of J. Reuben Clark.

In 1934, the council also established the first of its own committees, this one to deal with the wholesale repudiation of the Cuban Public Works bonds. Initially, the council had disclaimed any interest in undertaking direct negotiations on specific issues,[86] but under Clark, that policy faded. He believed, perhaps at the insistence of the bankers, that if the council did not form committees in cases such as Cuba, private independent groups would evolve to muddy the waters and confuse chances for an adjustment.[87] The idea for the Cuban committee, for example, arose because of the close ties between the council and the Chase National Bank, which had underwritten the $40 million in 5.5 percent bonds in

1930.[88] In the establishment of this committee, Clark set strict standards for memberships—bondholders who had no other motive for gain but the revitalization of their holdings.[89] There subsequently arose some suspicion that the council created its committee only to stop an independent committee then in the works.[90] This lent support to the claim that the council had subordinated itself to the banks, who wanted to eliminate attacks upon their integrity typically emanating from independent groups.

On November 15, 1934, a memorandum went out to the directors of the council stating that Clark had agreed to stay at the helm indefinitely. "It was not found possible to secure a person, satisfactory to all of the interests which had to be consulted, to take the place of Mr. Clark."[91] So the course was set. At the end of 1934, the council's first year, settlements had emerged in the Brazilian and Dominican situations, and negotiations were well underway with another six of the forty defaulting nations. J. Reuben Clark, Jr., had launched his assault on the Great Depression, and upon the emerging new order. His first truth was that there was indeed truth; there could be no change in eternal verities. As his own quest in defense of those verities, he had chosen the resurrection of the defaulted foreign bonds in America.

7

A Noise and a Shaking

So I prophesied as I was commanded: and as I prophesied,
there was a noise, and behold a shaking,
and the bones came together,
bone to his bone.

Reuben Clark boarded the Los Angeles Limited in Salt Lake City shortly after New Year's Day, 1935, heading back to New York and his work on the Foreign Bondholders Protective Council. Four months had expired since his self-imposed deadline for a termination of his service, but he had discovered that the mantle of the council presidency rested comfortably upon his shoulders. The Great Depression wore on, and Clark could not assume a passive role. The economic dysfunction had, in the midst of the New Deal and more radical threats from the left and right, become a great social tribulation that threatened to grind to dust the very foundation of the New Zion, the Constitution of the United States. He would take his place in the defenders' battle line as a soldier for international economic responsibility, and hence for the stabilization of the American system and the dimensions of the universe he knew. "Great masses of people everywhere in the world are wandering aimlessly . . . without any guiding principles," he lamented. "Every wind of doctrine strains the moorings that have held them for generations. This must be changed."[1] His devotion to the resurrection of American foreign bondholdings would be his badge of service in the great conflict.

Through the glass of his nineteenth-century spectacles, Clark could see his challenge clearly before him. Faced with unilateral write-downs or continuing defaults, the FBPC could only hope to encourage borrowing nations to choose terms for servicing their debts that were likely to please lenders, and furthermore to see that such terms emerged from truly bilateral consultations. The council's job was to unify the creditor side of the table, never an easy task. But even with a monolithic creditor front and a willing debtor, the history of such discussions revealed an uneven set of results at best.[2] An avid reader and student of history, Clark was certainly aware as he rode the train eastward that cold January of 1935 that write-downs of foreign debt were the norm in previous debt crises, not the exception.[3] Although he accepted the notion of debt relief in some form as a carrot to induce debtor cooperation, he would hold the line on write-downs or write-offs in favor of such forebearing techniques as conversions and reamortizations.

Clark's first major action after resuming his prophesying upon the bones was to address the Bond Club of New York. Standing before the assemblage of financiers and speculators on January 16, 1935, he used straight language to assess the defaulted foreign bonds situation after a full year of council effort. His opening statement contained his now-routine deferment to impartiality: "I always try to disabuse any hope that may be raised about what I may say by telling audiences of this type at the beginning that I am not an economist, I am not a financier, I never bought a bond, I never sold one, and I never owned one."[4] Getting down to business, he described "a bond claim as the lowest possible order of international claim," depending almost totally upon the good will of the debtor. The most important element that must be present, he said, was not a capacity but a will to pay. "Promises to pay that are not enforceable, and I have said to you that in the last analysis war is the only sanction to enforce an obligation, such promises to pay depend upon the good-will of the promissor, and that, in the last analysis, is all there is to this international bond situation. You must find in the foreign government in default a willingness to meet its obligations. Until you do find that willingness you are relatively helpless unless you are prepared to undertake the doctrine of reprisals, and later war."[5]

In this speech, as in all of his discourses and writings on the foreign debt situation thus far, Clark appeared uninterested in discussing any part of the problem except from this hard-line perspective—debtors must feel a moral obligation to pay. In his mind, the debtors' predicament deserved little sympathy. He offered no recognition, for example, to the obvious fact that the Great Depression in the developed world had led to protectionism, drastically lower import quantities and prices, export subsidies, and a withering of financial flows—hence a drying up of foreign exchange in debtor countries.[6] His consistent concern was in finding a way to get the borrowed money back—squeezing the turnip for all the blood that was in it.

Clark's hard message then was simply that the debts must be collected, but no effective recourses were open to the creditor: law suits were useless, either in domestic or international tribunals; diplomatic pressure might help, but retortion, reprisal, and physical force (peaceful blockade or war) were impossible. In the end, reported Clark, the promises in a foreign bond depended on the good faith of the promissor, and all too often, that faith was sadly lacking. He closed by assuring the Bond Club that his council would apply as much moral pressure as it could muster. The debtors would fulfill their obligations to the American bondholders.[7]

The moral pressure Clark hoped to conjure up depended for strength largely upon two domestic elements—a unified protective effort and a firm alliance with the federal government. Reality never blessed either factor during 1934, and within the first months of 1935, a jagged rift had opened between the FBPC and the government under a concerted attack from other bondholders' protective interests. Max Winkler, for example, had not eased his assault on the council and was "sneaking around, tearing apart every settlement" in a last-ditch attempt to put Title II into effect.[8] It appeared that the proverbial little foxes would destroy the vine to get the grapes.

Evidence of the growing tension first surfaced in Congress, where an idea arose that would have removed from the council its most effective lever of persuasion—the restoration of credit. Jumping on the neutrality legislation bandwagon, Representative Harold Knutson of Minnesota introduced a bill on January 3, 1935, proposing a ban on the importation "of government securities of foreign countries which have defaulted in their contract obligations to the United States."[9] Realizing that such an act would spill the war-debt hysteria into the foreign bond arena, Clark appealed to the State Department against the Knutson bill, suggesting instead the inclusion in treaty negotiations of some provisions covering services on long-term obligations of debtor countries then in default. This would bring the problem into the realm of international rather than unilateral law.[10]

Although Cordell Hull opposed Knutson's idea anyway,[11] the issue added water to a rising tide of anti-council opinion in Washington. Inevitably, Hull and Roosevelt were growing increasingly impatient with the council's necessarily slow and cumbersome processes. A rumor had arisen that they were in favor of a change in the FBPC that would bring it under a government agency to endow it with new and larger powers. Although demonstrably untrue, such an idea fed into an increasingly volatile set of circumstances that by the end of February encouraged FBPC opponents to step up their attacks.[12] Fortunately, the council had defenders in the State Department,[13] and nothing of immediate import came of this flurry of misgivings on the Potomac over the whole debt issue, despite the administration's wishes for neutrality legislation.

Consistent with his style, Clark responded to these attacks by stiffening his rhetoric against defaulting creditors while carefully choosing not to react directly to FBPC detractors. Success would silence them better than any public debate. As part of this effort, he catalogued all of the "contentions of defaulting debtors" and composed tough responses to each. Essentially, their excuses fell into four categories—the loans were imposed upon the debtors, there had been corruption in the negotiations, the debtors did not have the capacity to pay, or the welfare of the debtor nation would suffer. Clark countered all of these objections with sympathetic but unwaivering rejections. In any case, he thundered, "the debtor governments have had the money and have spent it. They owe it and should repay it."[14] And although he firmly asserted his belief that a foreign securities issue was strictly "between a sovereign and his private foreign creditors,"[15] he had also decided that the U.S. government should do (and should have done) much more to "control public-offered expansion stocks, bonds, etc." and to "speed production and provide national assistance in marketing surplus."[16] Clark wanted the federal government *out* of all negotiations on defaults but *in* on whatever activities that might encourage more responsible lending and provide funds so debtors could service their securities.

Turning from such challenges at home, Clark took advantage of Chile's apparent willingness to legislate for the satisfaction of its public debt and opened a dialog by cable with the government of Arturo Alessandri. The Chileans wanted to ease their external debt responsibility with a unilateral settlement, but Clark persuaded them to send a mission to New York to negotiate with the council. He consequently began a discussion with the Chilean commissioners on March 12, 1935.[17] By the time Clark turned the negotiations over to Francis White and left for

Mormonism's annual conference on April 1, the commission and the council had exchanged memorandums, and it appeared that they could easily discover common ground.[18]

When Clark arrived in Utah on April 3, the hopeful Chilean situation had not buoyed his spirits as observers might have expected. He was noticeably gruff as he lamented over the failure of the Brazilians to meet payments on January 1, 1935, which they had promised with the decree of February 5, 1934.[19] Because of the Knutson bill issue, he also dwelt upon the wholesale European cancellation of war debts (completed the previous June). He attacked that "villainous" default on the basis of what seemed to him to be simple economics. The United States, he said, received little benefit from World War I, whereas nations such as France infused billions of dollars into their economies though their defaults to the United States. Less than one-third of America's $11 billion loan to the allies, he told his western audience, went for munitions; the rest sank into domestic economies.[20] Perhaps the best explanation for Clark's disturbed peace of mind was the knowledge that one of the council's largest financial backers, Speyer and Company, was about to withdraw its support, ostensibly because of dissatisfaction with how the council handled the tenuous Brazilian case. He had already returned to Speyer a $2,500 donation[21] and would later assert that he ejected the firm for trying to influence the council.[22]

Clark seemed thoroughly besieged as he mounted the pulpit in the Salt Lake Tabernacle to affirm solemnly to his Mormon followers that "the Constitution of the United States and my adherence to it and support of it is part of my religion."[23] By now, he was convinced that the federal government, under New Deal maxims, plotted a disastrous course for America—the destruction of the Constitution as translated into the credo of the old order.[24]

And it was an apprehensive Reuben Clark who subsequently hurried back to New York to deal with his council's woes. The Speyer incident had spurred forces hostile to the council to new action. Criticism against FBPC financing had grown so vicious that the Department of State urgently invited Clark and White to Washington for extensive discussions on the future of the council. Feis and Phillips in particular were worried that because the great bulk of the council's funding came from such financial institutions as Speyer, a resolution for an investigation was likely to appear on Capitol Hill.[25] Accordingly, Clark and White arrived at the State Department at 2:30 p.m. on April 17, 1935. They met in Phillips's office with the assistant secretary, Feis, Sumner Welles, Fredrick Livesey, and Edwin C. Wilson of the State Department, and (unexpectedly for the council officers) Joseph F. Kennedy and John J. Burns of the Securities and Exchange Commission. The SEC people requested complete access to FBPC files to conduct an investigation under the powers of Section 211 of the Securities Exchange Act of 1934.[26] The council had fallen under siege.

Clark and White left Washington at 5:00 p.m., doubtlessly sobered considerably by their experience at Foggy Bottom, but the two had no time for lamentation. The Chilean commissioners had determined to break off negotiations and return home for further instruction from their government. The council consequently assembled them at 90 Broad Street on the afternoon of April 22 so that Clark could inform them of points he felt to be important in any adjustment on the external public debt of Chile. Clark handed the Chilean delegates a general plan containing many concessions the council would accept. In his explanation, he made certain demands outside of Chilean law that tied the commissioners' hands. The two parties thus agreed on April 25 that the Chileans should indeed return home, but for a discussion of Clark's plan. The essence of the difficulty seemed to be in terms of interest, and the sides were leagues apart—Chile asking 1/2 percent, the council 6 to 7.5 percent.[27] The road upon which the Chilean negotiations were traveling seemed to stretch far beyond the horizon, but the council needed to put the best face possible on the situation. "In view of the laudable concern manifested by Chile in the matter of meeting her obligations to her creditors," read its concluding statement, the FBPC "believes that the better understanding resulting from the present exchange of views will facilitate in the near future an arrangement which is fair both to Chile and to the American bondholders."[28] With the SEC axe poised over the council's neck, a success with Chile would have been a welcome counterpoise, but it just did not happen.

After the exit of the Chileans, Clark turned his attention necessarily to the Washington confrontation.[29] On Friday, May 3, William O. Douglas of the Securities and Exchange Commission visited him in New York to ascertain the level of cooperation the commission might expect. Clark had apparently determined to make a great stand at the SEC hearings and defend the council publicly, for Douglas left the talk pleased about Clark's willingness to work with the commission. "I had a satisfactory talk with Mr. Clark in New York City yesterday," he wrote Phillips. "He has very kindly consented to give us complete access to the files of his Council. I am anxious to begin our study with that Council since this is at the apex of the whole situation."[30]

To negate this cordial beginning with the SEC, however, an ominous event then occurred that further diminished the council's standing in the State Department. White chose this excitable time to make an ill-conceived request for the council's inclusion upon a list to receive all official department communications that concerned the some forty defaulting nations. He was in effect asking the department to treat the FBPC as a government agency with a "need-to-know" on extremely confidential and sensitive matters.[31] Virtually all who reviewed his request reacted negatively. Comments included: "ill-considered in detail"; "inconsiderate in the generality and comprehensiveness of its request for past information"; an attempt to get the department to "quietly incorporate it into the family of Government departments"; "hastily drafted"; and "quite ambiguous."[32]

As a further measure of this slippage of confidence, a few days later Lawrence Hoover wrote to Welles complaining about a State Department referral of a holder of Colombian bonds to the FBPC "when it is doing nothing and has not the charge of Colombian bondholders."[33] Welles's reply was a good deal less defensive of its sanctioning of the council than had been the case: "If, in referring an inquirer to the Council the Department incidentally mentions that it is understood that the Council has interested itself in situations which are of especial concern to the enquirer, I do not see that such incidental phrases are prejudicial to anyone."[34] In spite of Clark's cordial start with the SEC, it thus appeared that the Roosevelt administration had lost much faith in its fledgling stepchild.

Early in June, Clark left the council once again in White's hands and journeyed to Utah to work on some pressing church matters and to spend the summer away from the foreign bondholders storm.[35] On the way, he stopped in Des Moines to address the Iowa Bankers Association. His speech betrayed no shortage of conviction in his fight to resurrect the bonds: "If an issue of domestic bonds goes sour, we still benefit by investment of the proceeds in this country. On the other hand, if a foreign bond issue is floated in this country, an interest and principal are not paid to our investors, it is a real loss of our national wealth. We are poorer in direct proportion to our failure to collect, and it affects our welfare and prosperity."[36]

But the council had to admit that it was not gaining ground on the default situation—dollar issues were going into default or becoming past due faster than the FBPC could get negotiations underway on those that had been in default for some time.[37] To remedy this, the council, under White, pushed hard through the summer of 1935 to get talks underway with all of the defaulting states. By the time Clark returned to New York in mid-August, negotiations had resumed with Chile,[38] and new dialogues had opened with Argentina (Province of Buenos Aires), Czechoslovakia (City of Carlsbad), Guatemala, and Costa Rica.[39] In addition, the council made or continued contacts with several other debtor states, working with a total of eighteen defaulting governments.[40] This amounted to almost half of the states in some stage of default on their dollar obligations.

As before in Clark's absence, White's handling of the incendiary FBPC-government spat was somewhat less than spectacular. Noting that two new independent committees on Chile had formed, he complained to Feis that the State Department was the cause for the confusing and detrimental multiplication of protective groups. The FBPC was very effective, he claimed, but "its difficulties result chiefly from the fact that, while formed under Government auspices, its official standing has never been explicitly revealed." The department should therefore announce unequivocally in favor of a single committee (under the good offices of the council) for each defaulting country.[41] In an extremely cool response, Feis said that the department could not restrict the rights of other committees to form. "However, I confidently expect," he continued, "that experience will so clearly establish the ascendency, the ability, and the disinterested purposes of the Council as to make the problem of rival committees of diminishing importance as time goes on."[42] He was politely telling White that it would be up to the council alone to eliminate its troublesome competition.

No doubt exacerbating all of these difficulties were partisan and personal dynamics. For his part, White had the uncomfortable habit of addressing department officers with their first names, trying to force a familiarity that did not sit well in Washington. He would write, for example, to "Herbert" or "Wilbur," and receive curt answers addressed to "Mr. White."[43]

While White repeatedly committed faux pas that estranged the council from the administration in Washington, Clark's growing criticisms of the New Deal in speeches and correspondence inevitably rankled loyal Democrats in the State Department as much as it did those in Utah.[44] Occasionally, he launched forth against FDR's conduct of foreign policy, and this certainly won him no friends at Foggy Bottom. "Certainly not in my time, and I doubt if in any other time, there has been such a condition of flabby impotence brought into international relations the world over as exists at the present time and all because some people (I am naming no names . . .) have built a house of cards out of some impracticable ideas, from the League of Nations up or down, whichever way the gamut goes."[45]

Clark spent some six weeks in New York through August and September. Besides the ongoing correspondence and talks with the eighteen debtors with whom the council had opened channels, the executive committee was busy preparing for the SEC hearings over the council scheduled for the end of October.[46] Clark also occupied himself with personal appeals for financial support. In his letter to the directors, for example, he noted that they had contributed $1,275 during 1934, but to date in 1935, the council had received subscriptions from the directors in the amount of only $75.[47] To say the least, Clark found the council in the midst of compounding troubles.[48] And he did not try to conceal his mood at the pulpit of the Mormon conference in Salt Lake City in October. "It seems sometimes as if the darkness that surrounds us is all but impenetrable," he lamented. "I can see on all sides the signs of one great evil master and mind working for the overturning of our civilization, the destruction of religion, the reduction of men to the status of animals. This mind is working here and there and everywhere."[49] Of course, his siege mentality did not grow solely out of his troubles in New York. He was appalled at both foreign and domestic trends, abhorring fascism and welfarism equally.[50]

By October 15, the SEC had nearly completed its preparations for the hearings over the FBPC. It had also proposed to investigate Winkler, Lavis, Hoover, and the other people and organizations who claimed some authority in the foreign debt default issue.[51] On October 22, the SEC announced that a public hearing to examine the council and the other protective groups would commence Wednesday, October 30.[52] The SEC panel would consist of William O. Douglas (then director of the protective committee study, later chairman of the SEC), Samuel O. Clark, Jr., Abe Fortas, and Francis F. Lincoln.[53]

On the appointed day, Clark and White arrived at the commission's hearing room at 120 Broadway in New York and seated themselves at the witness table. Douglas opened the proceedings by reading into the record a long list of the financial institutions that supported the council monetarily, "including bankers and security dealers in every large city in the nation."[54] He then read the White House statement of October 20, 1933, which said that the council was to have no connections of any kind with the investment banking houses that originally issued the loans. Clark responded by drawing a distinction between the bank and the house of issue. He admitted that often the issue house was a subsidiary or in some other way connected to the banking house, but that "the original plans of the Council specifically provided for contributions from banks. And I want to say that the word 'connections' as used by the White House, means that these houses would have nothing to say to the way we conducted our business, then we are within the White House statement."[55] He repeated that despite charges to the contrary, houses of issue did not influence the council. They had, however, cooperated completely. Douglas asked Clark if a contributor might influence the council. Clark again quickly denied even the possibility: "If I did that, I would consider myself dishonest."[56] And so during the first days of the hearings, Clark deported himself quite well, sparring easily with Douglas and coming forth with good-humored bursts of righteous indignation whenever the questioning touched upon his personal integrity. Inasmuch as he had run the council from the beginning, those occasions came often.

Through the first two weeks of November, Clark continued to occupy the chair, and the hearing slowly began to go the council's way. Douglas gave Clark every opportunity to defend the organization and to discuss virtually all aspects of the council's operation that had come under criticism. His testimony bared such things as plots by rival committees and others to disrupt the council, his summary expulsion of Speyer for attempts to influence the council, and his staunch and consistent defense of the council's mode of operation.[57] One might say that Clark's success was nothing short of amazing. By the time the hearing recessed on November 20, Clark had finished his term at the witness table, and as the subsequent SEC report would reveal, he had won the council's position on nearly every point. Douglas had become almost an ally, and while not willing to overlook the council's faults, he would attest to Clark's integrity and the noble purposes of the Foreign Bondholders Protective Council.[58]

With understandable relief, Clark left New York to spend the winter in Utah, where, once again, his ecclesiastical responsibilities beckoned him. He arrived in Salt Lake City on November 27, saying only that the council was "making progress in its efforts."[59] He said nothing to reporters about the difficulties that had so befraught the council in 1935.[60] In the meantime, the FBPC released over Clark's signature an announcement of a satisfactory settlement (for 75 percent of full interest payments) with the Province of Buenos Aires.[61] Clark requested that holders of the issues donate $1.25 for each $1,000 bond to the council, and asked that the Argentines to do the same. In this way, the council hoped to establish a better financial base and relieve its heavily criticized dependence upon financial institutions.[62]

On Friday, December 6, Reuben Clark addressed the Exchange Club at its annual convention in the Hotel Utah. The terse tenor of this speech marked it as the keynote in a new phase in his demeanor with regard to the foreign default situation—the "hard-fisted" part of the Feis sobriquet. Perhaps seeing the apparent SEC exoneration as something of a new mandate, Clark blasted many of the debtors for their unwillingness to pay, and in part blamed the foreign bond defaults for the continuation of the depression in the United States. After two years in the council presidency, and after all of the difficulties he had worked against, he had apparently decided to let the diplomatic front crumble in favor of a get-tough approach in public. He thus revealed his innermost conclusions and philosophies over the whole issue, none of which fared well for the debtors. Unlike domestic loans, Clark said, for every dollar loaned abroad and never realized upon, an equivalent amount of wealth was lost to the United States. He vigorously and unsympathetically attacked the debtors' flimsy excuses for nonpayment.

> Most of these nations today feel that in some manner they were forced to borrow this money, and now, after spending the money unwisely, feel no obligation to pay it back. We may have been unwise in some of these loans, but nevertheless we delivered 100 cents on the dollar. Had we even suggested that this country or a committee of the bondholders should supervise spending of the funds to prevent needless extravagance, it would have led to bitter resentment and ill feeling on the part of the debtors.
>
> When approached for a settlement of the bonds, representatives say, earnestly and soberly, they want to knock off 50 per cent of the debt. The Council feels that a nation may reasonably devote from 20 to 30 per cent of its revenues to servicing the public debt. Our government admits it is paying 28 per cent, while Great Britain,

France and Japan each are paying 40 per cent of their revenues to their debts. Yet some of the debtor nations seriously want to pay as little as 2.6 per cent of their income to payment of public debt.[63]

Clark closed this opening barrage in his new campaign with an assault upon debtor "boondoggling," which he defined as government extravagance in the face of public indebtedness—the building of hospitals, schools, jails, and "dining rooms for workers."[64] This theme would become a major element in the council's argument during the coming years.

A few days later, Clark lashed out at another debtor practice that raised his ire. Some of the debtor nations had discovered that they could buy up their own bonds that were selling at greatly depreciated prices because the governments were not paying service upon them.[65] In this way they were diverting funds and foreign exchange that should have gone to interest or sinking fund payments to the purchase of their own devaluated bonds on the open market. Clark indicted the obligors for this "immoral" attempt to relieve themselves of their external debt burdens. With great disgust, he advised Utahns and all Americans never to invest abroad again.[66] "Generous America has found out," he would subsequently muse, "that the person or government toward whom one is being generous can always exceed his benefactor's generosity with the latter's money."[67]

His new aggressiveness on the bond issue notwithstanding, Clark settled into a church project even closer to his passions. Mormon authorities had become so incensed over the government "dole" that they determined the church would take all of its members off the welfare roles and "take care of its own." Reuben Clark naturally wanted a forward place in this task. He set the end of 1936 as the goal for having the estimated eighty-eight thousand needy Saints completely out of government relief programs. This would require a massive machinery and a strain upon the church's fewer than a million members, but the Mormon hierarchy had to overcome the "evils of the dole."[68] Clark thus spent the winter months fighting the social revolution of the thirties in a way apart from the foreign bond business but in every sense closer to his beliefs.

Clark remained in Salt Lake City until the April conference of the church, with the exception of a publicity visit to Alf Landon in Topeka, where he predicted that Landon would easily receive the Republican nomination for the presidency.[69] To suggest that Clark would have been delighted with an appointment as secretary of state is to suggest the obvious.[70] He then journeyed once again to New York to join White in the foreign securities crusade. He nevertheless continued to devote extensive effort to the Mormon welfare plan. On Sunday evening, May 24, he spoke at the Mormon chapel at 76th Street and Broadway in Manhattan. Having given notice of his speech to the press, Clark spoke to almost as many reporters as he did Mormons. He announced ambitious plans for getting all members of the church off the welfare roles by October 1, 1936. The money, he said, would come from two sources—tithing and a "fast offering" in which Mormons would contribute the cost of two meals from which they would abstain on a fast day once a month. Estimating the cost of the "Church Security System" at more than $1 million a year, Clark believed that the Latter-day Saints could accomplish the task for about 45 percent of the government's cost of caring for the same people. The Mormons would do it "without pay and for love." The already-existent ecclesiastical system of lay bishops and "home teachers" would administer the program that would take the Mormons first off home relief and then off work relief. Afterward, they would work in church welfare projects on farms and in canneries. As he summarized the Mormon position, "Not many years ago, the Church did take care of its own people, but then somehow it slipped away and on the theory that we were taxpayers and supporting the burden of caring for the needy, we began sending them to poorhouses. The presidency of the Church feels that it is time that we got back to first principles and cared for our own. That is the task we have set for ourselves this Summer."[71]

Reuben Clark intended to engage the enemies of the old order on two fronts. For America, he would break the siege on the council, and he would continue to raise up the dry bones of defaulted foreign securities and of international responsibility. And for his community of Mormons, he would, as Moses of old, lead them out of the bondage of the New Deal. The old universe could not pass without a struggle.

CHAPTER

8

Prophesying upon the Bones

And when I beheld,
lo, the sinews and the flesh came up on them,
and the skin covered them above:
but there was no breath in them.

On Monday, December 30, 1935, the SEC hearings on the Foreign Bondholders Protective Council resumed in the New York office of the commission at 120 Broadway, with the council's vice president, Francis White, testifying. Within a few days, White had finished his term in the chair, and while the SEC scrutinized other protective efforts, the council anxiously awaited the decision of William O. Douglas and his panel. With the literal survival of the council hanging in the balance, many of the organization's opponents (and many Washington officials) had come to believe that the Title II concept might be a much better idea after all, because it would receive its funding from an agency such as the Reconstruction Finance Corporation (RFC) rather than Wall Street. The recommendation of the Douglas panel would tip the balance.[1]

During the course of the hearing, the panel also looked carefully into other bondholders' organizations, particularly those aspiring to supplant the council. Hoover, Winkler, Lavis, and the others all appeared before the panel. Bankers, institutional bondholders, and any other interests in the defaults also testified about their connections and the experiences in the entire situation, but the discussion focussed upon the FBPC, no matter who occupied the chair.[2]

Thinking that the council might be down for the count, rival protective groups increased their attacks upon its sovereignty in the field of default negotiations. In April 1936, for example, the FBPC asked holders of Colombian bonds to file their names, addresses, and the amounts of their holdings. The council would then keep them advised of any developments in its negotiations with Bogota.[3] Within days, a Hoover-inspired consortium calling itself the Bondholders Committees for the Republic of Colombia threatened the council officers with a law suit to restrain them from "injecting" themselves into the Colombian bond situation.[4] Hoover battered away at the FBPC for not protesting Colombian payments on short-term credits to the same issue houses that "controlled" the council. He hoped to create a picture of scheming bankers bilking long-term investors in order to keep up the payments on high-interest, short-term credits.[5]

Not only were the little foxes nipping at the council's heals. Its efforts in all directions increasingly encountered noncooperation, distrust, and general obstruction. Many truly concerned individuals and institutions refused to associate with the FBPC because of the taint from charges that the issue houses controlled the organization through financial pressure. These generally honest and sincere people entered the campaign against the council because of five basic suspicions: (1) The council had not enough technical skill and lacked aggressive qualities; (2) it permitted other creditors to take precedence over bondholders; (3) it was controlled by bankers, hence protected their interests first; (4) it did not concern itself with claims against the houses; and (5) "There is the charge that these and related weaknesses and defects of the Council are traceable to the control which investment bankers exercise over it . . . as a result of the subtle influences of Wall Street."[6]

In spite of this deepening trouble and the trauma of awaiting the SEC decision on life or death, the council began to exert more vigorous pressure for the revitalization of the defaulted bonds. And the mood of the effort changed noticeably. Clark, White, and other officers struck out more frequently at the unwillingness of the debtors to service their debts. Although it was impossible to quantify the effect of the council's woes upon the defaulters, apparently the executive committee decided that a hard-line approach could not hurt their probably already low standing with debtors. Thus the unlimited war Clark had declared at the end of 1935 grew hotter through the summer of 1936, and the council would soon overcome at least the charges that it lacked the aggressive muscle required to attack the slacking governments for their "immoralities" in meeting external debt obligations.

In the meantime, FBPC officers continued a cautious policy of refusing to advise individual bondholders about when to unload depreciated holdings. "With reference to your question as to the holding or selling these bonds," Clark told one troubled soul, "the Council never gives any advice of this sort."[7] They also tempered their sympathies. "I am very sorry that you lost your money," Clark wrote another sorrowing investor, "and hope you followed the rule that one must not speculate with money which one is not prepared to lose."[8] Still, the council recognized that if bondholders en masse were to unload their securities at depreciated prices, it had lost the war no matter what it did. As a result, Clark *was* willing to offer the following kind of "nonadvice":

> I think if I held the bonds and were not in a position where I was under the necessity of selling these bonds or some others, I should not sacrifice them at these rates but gamble that there might be an improvement. I would do this not on the basis of any specific information which I have but merely because it seems to me that conditions in Europe are about as bad as they can get, (short of another great war, which may come), and, therefore, the chances are at least even that the bonds may improve in price in the next months. In making such a decision for myself I would understand that I might be wholly wrong and the bonds might go down to nothing.[9]

In their communication with and about the debtors, Clark and the others exercised no such caution. They took every opportunity to blast those states that were repatriating their own depreciated securities with funds they should have devoted to bringing the same issues out of default.[10] In support of this point, the council first backed federal legislation that would make it a felony for anyone to deal in such repatriation schemes.[11] Then, believing themselves on firm legal ground, they also made an effort to eliminate the "capacity to pay" excuse from the private foreign debt situation. This concept, they claimed, was valid only in intergovernmental obligations because the dealings were between sovereign equals who could justly bargain on such a point. According to the creed of the council, sovereigns who borrowed from private parties should know whether they would be able to pay. Hence, it was all a matter of will to pay. With astonishing callousness, Clark maintained further that international law demanded that "the whole wealth of the nation, including the private wealth of all the nationals of that nation, is subject to tax up to extinction for the debts of the sovereign."[12]

Under yet another tack, Clark condemned the practice of many debtors of allowing default while spending large sums on extravagant "public works projects . . . such as the building of expensive scenic roads through mountains, palatial and luxurious public buildings, highly ornamental boulevards and avenues, etc., etc., etc."[13] At least he had removed schools and hospitals from the list, but he still classified the practice as unsound and unjustified both in questions of fiscal policy and morality.[14] In brief, the council required debtors to place their external obligations near the very top of their list of revenue priorities. A fourth major council complaint against the debtors involved what it classified as "bondholdings bought below par." In this case, the debtor would claim that the present holders of its bonds purchased them at greatly reduced prices, so the obligor had no responsibility to service them at full value. The FBPC denied this idea first on the grounds that the great bulk of the defaulted bonds were still in the hands of the people of modest means who had purchased them originally and were in danger "of losing everything they have saved during a lifetime, if their bonds are not paid."[15] In the second place, said the council, the unpaid foreign bond amounted to an equivalent loss in the national wealth of the creditor. "If a foreign government were to borrow one dollar and then pay back only twenty cents, on the theory that the present holder of its obligation had paid only twenty cents for it, and therefore no more should be paid to the holder to wipe out the obligation, the national wealth involved in the investment would be depleted by eighty per cent."[16] The foreign dollar debtors must therefore pay their obligations in full no matter what the depreciated value.

The final weapon in the council's arsenal consisted of its outspoken resistance to the idea that inasmuch as the interest rate at the time the loan was made was too high, the interest rate should have scaled down as the current rate went down. The borrower and the lender, retorted the FBPC, took the risk that the rate might change up or down with time. No lender would dare claim that the interest on his or her loan should increase with an upward change in rate.[17] Clark and the council would no longer entertain excuses. The time had come for a reckoning, depression or not.

After a summer of intense negotiations with several debtors (particularly Cuba, Colombia, and El Salvador), Reuben Clark again handed the baton to White and the council's increasingly savvy secretary A. Helen Wylie before heading west to work on the Mormon welfare system.[18] On October 7, 1936, he outlined the progress of the Church Security Plan in

the Salt Lake Tabernacle. He admitted that fulfillment of the plan had
been slow, but he declared that the world was watching the Saints for an
alternative to the New Deal. In spite of this slight exaggeration, Clark's
discussion of the plan realistically called for a new communitarianism
among Mormons to avoid the evils attendant to the government dole.
Mormon philosophies of thrift, hard work, and independence, he said,
must now revolve about the concepts of love and self-sacrifice for the
well-being of the Saints. The plan, Clark continued, was a revelation from
God. It would work, and no Mormon would accept money from Washington, and no Mormon would want for the necessities of life.[19]

With the defeat of Alf Landon in November, Clark's dream of heading
the State Department disappeared as did his fervent hopes for a quick and
easy demise of the New Deal.[20] But the foreign bond battle still beckoned,
so after Christmas, he boarded the eastbound train again. Within a few
days of his arrival "home," his British counterpart Sir Otto Niemeyer
(who was also a director of the Bank of England) landed in New York,
announcing that he had come to discuss the international financial
situation with the American group. Although the FBPC had scheduled no
conference with Niemeyer, it would be happy to meet with him. Sporting
the archetypal bowler hat and a thin moustache on his stiff upper lip,
Niemeyer indicated a desire to get some coordinated effort underway. "I
am here for one purpose, to meet with the American bondholders, to
survey the situation and see if some way can be found to remedy it."[21] He
subsequently paid a so-called courtesy call at 90 Broad Street.[22] But for
three weeks, Sir Otto's visit was anything but a courtesy call. He and
Clark talked daily, either at the council's offices or in Niemeyer's suite at
the Biltmore Hotel. At the end of that period, Clark announced a new era
of cooperation rather than competition between the various national
protective organizations, and in particular those of the United States and
Great Britain. There would be no formal agreements, but rather increased
contacts that would "enable the two groups to cooperate where they have
common interests."[23] Because of his pacifism, Clark must also have been
pleased with Niemeyer's prediction of "detente in Europe, no war."[24]

Despite the incidental nature with which the council clothed these talks
in the press, their meaning was clear. Clark was moving to clear away all
objections to the council, such as that it had destroyed the former aura of
cooperation between creditor nations with its intense championing of the
dollar-bond cause.[25] With this intent, and while still awaiting the all-
important SEC report, Clark cancelled the annual meeting of members

(scheduled for February) in favor of a subsequent special conference to discuss the financial affairs of the organization: "The matter of replenishment of the General Fund requires careful consideration. However, the Executive Committee and Officers of the Council feel that this matter may be most profitably considered after the SEC has made its report upon the investigation of the Council which it conducted last year. This report has apparently been delayed for some months, though press reports from Washington indicate it may be expected in the near future."[26]

In the meantime, criticism of the council's financing continued unabated. A nasty but good example of this ongoing denunciation occurred in late February and early March. It began when the government of Poland announced that, as a result of its talks with the council, it was willing to resume service on three issues but at greatly reduced rates. Clark expressed his dissatisfaction with the Polish offer, but he was convinced it was the best the council could obtain at the moment.[27] This acceptance ignited a campaign in the *New York Post* to discredit the council completely. The pro-New Deal, anti-Wall Street paper charged that, in effect, Clark had taken a bribe from Poland, because his acceptance of the Polish offer would enrich the council's coffers.[28] A *Post* correspondent even telephoned Newton Baker in Cleveland and accused him of being an unwitting pawn of the issue houses.[29]

Uncharacteristically, Clark decided to meet the *Post* challenge directly and personally. He arranged an interview with its reporter, a Mr. Saada, and after forty minutes with him on March 3, 1937, believed that he had explained the council's position satisfactorily.[30] To his chagrin, the paper then printed a broadside that accused the council of a "$30,000 take" for getting $69 million in "Nazi bonds" on the SEC register.[31] What the paper so flagrantly misrepresented were funding bonds of coupons of middle- and long-term, non-Reich obligations that the council managed to induce the Germans to register in 1936.[32] The $30,000 figure would have been the council's customary one-eighth percent donation from bondholders and Germany, most of which, of course, never came in. The *Post* evidently had advance notice of a council announcement on the German 3 percent funding bond offer on March 8, 1937, which culminated an effort Clark had begun on May 29, 1934, to get the German bonds registered.[33] No doubt frustrated and unamused, Clark apparently decided that this marked a fine time to put in some time on his church duties in Utah. Fighting the devil might be easier than grappling further with the intractable *Post*.[34]

During his absence, and as the imminence of the SEC report grew,

White expressed apprehension to his friend Feis over the possibility that the Douglas panel would recommend a reversion to the Title II concept. He fully expected that the council could get foundations to come to its aid if only the SEC would refrain from requiring public financing.[35] Despite such worries, when the long-awaited report emerged on May 14, 1937, it filled the best hopes of the council's officers and endorsed the FBPC as "the appropriate permanent agency" to protect American holders of foreign bonds. One paragraph in particular thrilled Clark, who had returned to New York in the middle of April:

> The Council was organized at the suggestion and on the initiative of the Government. During its existence it has shown a record of constructive endeavor despite limitations and handicaps. It has functioned economically; it has been free of entrepreneurial influences; and it has brought about a resumption of debt service on a number of defaulted issues. It has maintained a quasi-public character, and those who have served as directors and members of its executive committee have not been actuated by mercenary motives but by a sense of public service.[36]

The panel, as expected, also made extensive suggestions for the modification of the council's financial arrangement, but it happily left the execution of these reforms to the organization itself, and it did not suggest any reversion to the Title II concept of funding. The Douglas panel recommended the ouster from membership of all houses of issue, fiscal agents, short-term creditors, holders of commercial credits of foreign property interests, brokers, dealers, and their attorneys, with all financing completely independent of these groups.[37] Inasmuch as these recommendations would eliminate more than 60 percent of the council's financial base, some observers believed that its officers would react adversely to the report, but the reverse was true.[38] The SEC had "canonized" the council,[39] more than Clark and the others might have dreamed possible. They could solve the financial problem, although at the moment it was probably worse than anyone supposed. The 205 contributing members had paid $80,182 in 1936. By the end of 1937, the number of contributing members had dropped to sixty-nine, and their donations totaled only $1,517.[40]

Clark and White immediately began efforts to meet the SEC requirements. They made numerous inquiries to the State Department, the SEC, and others in Washington in order to make certain the council understood the recommendations and was able to fill them completely.[41] The Douglas panel had recommended a federal loan of perhaps $1 million to tide the organization over until other financing began to materialize. Clark wanted very much to stave off this notion, "not from fear that the lending authority would attempt to control the Council but because the Council would be brought under great pressure from politicians."[42] On June 28, he flew to Washington for a conference on this matter and others at the State Department.[43] During a chat with Douglas between meetings at State, Clark raised an ugly issue that must have made the liberal Douglas wince. As Clark remembered,

> I wished to make an observation, but I had great difficulty in framing it so as not to seem to mean more than I wished to mean. I wished to express personally and confidentially as between us that I should like to assure him that we must look with greatest care upon anyone whom we took into our organization. There has been a persistent effort by certain Jewish firms ever since the Council was organized to get someone here in the Council. I am not trying to conduct a pogrom, but I am merely commenting on a fact, and saying that we must be most careful as to anyone whom we might take in. Commissioner Douglas indicated that we would have to be tremendously careful.[44]

And we must be tremendously careful here. Although Clark privately and occasionally in public made no secret about his anti-Semitism and related racist attitudes,[45] this cautious remark to Douglas does not by itself indicate that the council under his leadership made important decisions based upon racial or ethnic prejudice. Certainly his trepidation over the power of a Jewish banking combination fit his conservative viewpoint and was not unusual on Wall Street at the time.

After a busy day of conferences in Washington, Clark returned to New York, convinced that he then knew exactly what to do. He issued a call for a directors' meeting on July 13, 1937, to enact amendments to the council's bylaws.[46] On the appointed day, the full membership met in New York, where Clark presented his proposed amendments. The directors voted unanimously to adopt these reforms that (1) set higher standards for membership that eliminated (almost) every hint of conflict of interest; (2) reduced the board of directors "to more workable proportions"; (3) placed limitations on officers' salaries; and (4) provided for the annual publication of a financial statement and independent scrutiny by a "Board of Visitors" from Washington.[47]

Following this meeting, Clark requested that the administration quickly form the Board of Visitors and forward copies of the amended bylaws to Cordell Hull and Douglas. He further asked that the department and the commission as soon as possible make an announcement that the FBPC was, by virtue of its conformity to government desires, "in very deed the central authority which the Commission in its Report expressed the belief the Council should become."[48] Clark was to leave for Berlin to negotiate with Schacht over the German dollar bond case on July 15, and he hoped that the government's endorsement of the council would precede him to Europe to enhance his authority. The SEC, however, was still not sure that the council deserved such a statement, because the FBPC had granted immunity from the effects of the amendments to the original directors. Nevertheless, the commission was willing, short of an open endorsement, to let the issue slide until those effected directors came up for reelection.[49] Consequently, on July 21, 1937, the Securities and Exchange Commission and the Department of State announced de facto government support for the council by agreeing to designate a Board of Visitors consisting of Feis and Douglas to examine the organization's finances and incidental operations periodically.[50] Wanting an unequivocal federal endorsement to silence its critics, the council was not completely satisfied, but it appeared that the siege had broken, and that the organization had secured its survival.[51]

As planned, Clark sailed from New York for Europe on board the *Bremen* on July 15, 1937. The purpose of his journey was threefold: First, he would tour the Mormon missions in Europe along with eighty-one-year-old Heber Grant, president of the church.[52] During the course of the trip, he would also hold conferences in Berlin with Reichsbank officials. Finally, he would attend meetings of the Committee for the Study of International Loan Contracts under the auspices of the Finance Committee of the League of Nations and visit the bondholders' protective associations in Belgium, France, Britain, the Netherlands, and Switzerland. White would follow up with a trip to London in December for a conference of national protective organizations.[53] These journeys symbolized the major policy shift that criticisms of the past months had forced upon Clark. There could be no more isolationism in international debt settlement. He would cooperate with the League of Nations, and he would go also to Hitler's Berlin. With the SEC battle won, he apparently could taste total victory and was willing to take personally uncomfortable steps to achieve it.[54]

When Clark and Grant returned from Europe, they turned their attentions to an apparent miracle in the Great Basin. In a modern replay of Genesis 41, it seemed that God had provided a bumper crop in the Rockies to shore up the Saints against the coming world crisis that Clark had prophesied the previous April. The Mormons thus called a special fast day to raise funds with which to build a great storehouse in Utah to contain the plenty, and bishops in all Sunday services read two paragraphs from Clark's April prognosis:

> Within the next few years we shall, in the normal course, suffer a depression far more serious, affecting intimately far greater numbers of people, than the one we are now finishing.
>
> To prepare for this coming disaster we must avoid debt as we would avoid a plague. Let us live strictly within our incomes and save a little money. Let every head of every household have on hand enough food and clothing and fuel for at least a year ahead. Do not speculate.[55]

This greater depression never came, but Clark's advice remains to this day a prime maxim of practical Mormonism.

Clark's speech a few days later at the October Mormon conference illuminated further his feelings of foreboding, and again his worldview: "I am grateful, also, as I return to this country, for our country itself. I am grateful for its territorial aloofness from the rest of the world. Even with the most modern, destructive weapons of war, we are almost immune. I am grateful for our political international aloofness and I pray our Heavenly Father that we shall never lose the security which comes from minding our own business and remaining aloof from the quarrels and the pettiness of the politics of the world."[56] But he saw grave danger even in America's great blessings: "I am grateful for our economic sufficiency—that we can, within our own borders, produce all that we need for our daily lives, and the most of what we need for our luxury. The need of other great powers for this sufficiency threatens to bring sometime in the future another devastating struggle."[57]

Having thus discharged his duties as "one of the Lord's annointed," Clark returned to New York in order to receive the new Board of Visitors on its first annual inspection of the council's finances.[58] After indicating that they would visit after Christmas,[59] Douglas and Feis came to 90 Broad Street on December 17, 1937, spent several hours examining the records of the council and interviewing its officers, then returned to

Washington. "As I remember it, we went up to New York . . . to lunch and talk with the officers of the council," Feis wrote. "Their administration of the organization was admirable and their finances modest, though the officers were well-enough paid. However, rightly or wrongly, I got the sense that the less often we visited their shop the more welcome we would be."[60] For his part, hoping that the board's findings would add to the council's ascendancy, Clark entrained for the West and Christmas on his Utah ranch.[61]

No sooner had he arrived home than good news concerning his organization's fight for hegemony in foreign bond negotiations developed from another sector. In November, the council had begun discussions with Yugoslavia. Now, two independent committees concerned with Yugoslavian issues announced that they were completely confident that the FBPC was capable of handling ably all negotiations with that country, and that they would consequently deactivate in deference to the council.[62] This symbol of achievement notwithstanding, Clark continued to await the board's report hopefully. Finally, on January 8, 1938, the State Department and the SEC published the letter that Feis and Douglas had submitted to their respective agencies concerning the two men's visit to the council. They drew a dreary picture of the foreign bond situation in general, but at the same time they praised the council for its earnest activity in behalf of American bondholders. They also recommended that the administration abandon permanently the idea of a government agency to do the job of the council.[63]

The positive tenor of the report was particularly satisfying to Reuben Clark. As he boarded the Los Angeles Limited for another trip to New York, he luxuriated in his delight "that the report has been made in such favorable terms."[64] His sturdy defense of the council during four years of service as its president was beginning to pay dividends. We can only imagine his sense of satisfaction and accomplishment.

The happy effects of the positive SEC report of the previous May multiplied rapidly after the release of the letter. Perhaps even more important than the many committees now willing to bow to the council's sovereignty was the fact that the gaping rift with the administration had begun to narrow considerably. For example, the State Department in January made a subtle but important change in its formula for replying to bondholders so enquirers would not feel that the council was without government sanction and support. "In letters to bondholders instead of saying 'since the Council functions entirely independently of the Government, reference is made to it without responsibility on the part of this Department' we use a formula: 'The Council functions on its own responsibility, and reference to it is made without responsibility on the part of this Department.'"[65] In addition, the department began to ignore completely the continuing attacks from such die-hard critics as Winkler and Hoover.[66] By the early spring of 1938, the council's long-standing troubles with Washington thus appeared to have come to a virtual end.

The FBPC's annual report for 1937 reflected its sense of satisfaction not only in terms of its improved relationship with the government and its successful struggles for hegemony, but also in the achievements at negotiations during the year. "In the course of the year," it noted, "the Council has been occupied with 26 default situations, in 20 countries, involving 254 different bond issues, with a total face value of approximately 1.8 billion dollars."[67] Almost miraculously, Clark and his colleagues had "arranged two temporary adjustments with Poland involving eight bond issues, two permanent settlements with China involving two different issues, and one permanent settlement with Uruguay involving four issues."[68] It also declared three other negotiations as nearly concluded and attacked with new boldness "immoral" debtor practices, in particular the repatriation maneuver.[69]

Then, at long last, Clark received a letter dated May 10, 1938, from Douglas, now chair of the Securities and Exchange Commission, that signaled with finality the council's victory over the current of troubles and criticisms that it had struggled against since its inception. Douglas confirmed officially the council's total conformity to the standards the commission had set in its report: "These statutory changes have been a source of great satisfaction to the Commission. We believe [the Council's] action in so promptly adopting the suggestions for improving its own high standards is worthy of highest commendation."[70] He concluded by conveying the SEC's "approval of the amendments to the Council's By-Laws to which I have referred and of the manner by which the Council has complied with the recommendations contained in the above-mentioned report of this Commission to Congress."[71]

Shortly thereafter, the New York Stock Exchange for the first time agreed to cooperate with the council in bringing pressure to bear upon a defaulting debtor (Chile).[72] The Foreign Bondholders Protective Council, after four and a half years of burdensome strife and disunity in the business of representing American bondholders, finally had achieved its coveted legitimacy and its effectively unchallenged hegemony.

J. Reuben Clark, Jr., the council's great moving force from its beginning, surveyed this apparently triumphant scene and determined that he
could no longer justify his service to two masters. Accordingly, he
relinquished the mantle of the council presidency and gave up his trans-
continental commuting in favor of a more settled existence as a Mormon
prelate. "When at the invitation of your Executive Committee," he wrote
in his letter of resignation, "I became acting President of the Council at
the end of February 1934, it was with the definite understanding that my
services should not extend for a longer period than six months. Various
causes, unnecessary to recapitulate here, have lengthened that time to the
present."[73] His friend Francis White became president, and Clark, unable
to give up the cause completely, accepted election as chair of the executive
committee.[74] For after all, what would be the prophesying without the
prophet?

9

Prophesying unto the Wind

Then he said unto me, Prophesy unto the wind,
prophesy, son of man, and say to the wind,
Thus saith the Lord God; Come from the four winds,
O breath, and breathe upon these slain,
that they may live.

Immediately after retiring from the council presidency, Reuben Clark undertook one more serious mission in behalf of people who held foreign bonds. In June of 1938, and with the title of chair of the executive committee, he returned to Europe for another session with the Germans. Because of *Anschluss* in March, the Austrian external debt was now in complete default along with that of the intransigent Germans. Clark's work in Nazi Berlin, however, bore no fruit. He then went to Paris for another meeting of the several national bondholders' organizations as a part of the league's Committee for the Study of International Loan Contracts.[1] This would be his last major effort for the council.[2] His calling in Salt Lake City must now take precedence over the work of the FBPC.

As he traveled home to Utah, Clark carried with him an unhappy sense both of the European situation he had just observed firsthand and of the continuing "excesses" of the New Deal. With his great success in establishing the council's potency, Clark had begun to agonize with increased intensity over the imminence, first of all, of international disaster. He could sense the forces about to draw the United States into war in Europe. Hitler's hunger for *Liebensraum* appalled the Utah pacifist, but Clark also viewed with great trepidation the "hate propaganda" that promised to "overwhelm the world in another world war,"[3] not the kind of hate the Nazis would employ to gain their ends but rather the self-righteous judgment of one nation upon the actions of another. He again addressed his Mormons from the pulpit of the Salt Lake Tabernacle:

I now beseech you, to consider whether or not we Americans who have gained the most of the land which we possess—including that on which we stand—by conquest, and whether or not the other great nations who have glutted themselves with the spoils of the conquest, are in a position to condemn without mitigation some other nation which is merely attempting to march along the way of empire which we and those other nations followed. I beseech you not to put yourselves nor this nation in the position of whited sepulchers. I loathe war, I loathe conquest, I loathe oppression, I loathe the destruction of the liberties of men; I love freedom, I love our free institutions, but let us not visit upon the people themselves the sins of their governments.[4]

Clothing the isolationist message in religious garb, he begged for peace and forebearance. "Rightousness and hate cannot dwell in the same heart, no matter how great the rightousness nor how little the hate."[5] His message was for Americans to aspire only to a position of moral force and to eschew the use of the sword. The actions of such as Hitler and Mussolini would not respond to the use of physical force. The lessons of World War I were plain: Neutrality and isolationism were the only course for the New Zion.

Free from his duty as a council representative to curry favor in Washington, Clark also unleashed a new fury against New Deal policies. In November 1938, for example, he attended a conference of the American Bankers Association in Houston, where to the dismay of the old guard, a pro-New Deal banker became vice president of the organization. In response to this blasphemous turn of events, the retiring president, a Mormon friend of Clark's named Orval W. Adams, attacked the fiscal policies of the government as leading to fascism. In another scathing address, Adam Bennion, another Mormon member of the association, added his disgust for Roosevelt's policies. Clark then capped the comments of his fellow Utahns by saying that the government was trying to become God. He further reminded the bankers of their "holy duty" to wage war on waste, extravagance, misuse of public funds, and demagoguery. He also spoke out vehemently against the income tax as a misguided attack on private property and an abusive administration attempt to redistribute the wealth.[6] This particular meeting of the ABA became something of a Mormon vendetta against the New Dealers, a replay of the Israelites to the Philistines.

The following summer, for another example, Clark blasted the new order at the Citizens Conference on Government Management at Estes Park, Colorado. "A planned and subsidized economy beats down initiative, wipes out industry, destroys character and prostitutes the electorate," according to Clark. "We Mormons have cared for the essential needs of our own in the past. We can do it now. We can do it in the future if we can be relieved of the debauchery to character which follows the dole."[7] At a meeting of the Association for Life Insurance Presidents that winter, he joined with J. W. Bricker of Ohio in criticizing Roosevelt and the New Deal for the reckless government expansion. In this context, Clark revealed his innermost feelings about the new age: "A nation-wide organization of informed policy holders would give short shift to all these slant-eyed schemes of designing revolutionists against the existing order, which has been born and bred of the wisdom of the ages and of the sacrifice and blood of your ancestors."[8] It was truly a struggle against the collapse of the old universe, and without the foreign bond forum to infuse his rhetoric with direction, Clark's resistance to the passing of the old order quickly became negative and less intellectually appealing.[9]

During the 1940s, Clark's extra-religious activities bent almost exclusively toward his great passions for neutrality and isolationism. The excesses of the New Deal took a back seat to the approaching war. Personally crushed over the death of a son-in-law at Pearl Harbor, he watched with foreboding sorrow as the United States entered World War II and spent the duration urging Americans to make the best of things by at least avoiding the mistakes that their involvement in World War I had fostered. Among these especially, he said, were the foolish foreign loans. As one of his last official acts before retiring as chair of the council's executive committee at the end of 1945, the seventy-four-year-old Clark made a last fervent appeal for the United States not to further loans to foreign governments. The sad experiences in foreign lending of the past, he pleaded, should eliminate the possibility of a repetition of error. Besides, "behind this plan for foreign loans with its outward humanitarianism is a subversive plot to make the whole world communistic on the Soviet plan."[10] His postwar devils also came to include the United

Nations ("a violation of American sovereignty") and NATO ("an entangling alliance").[11]

Into the fifties, the aged Clark grew more vehemently conservative and more anticommunist until his once potently careful set of beliefs had degenerated into a McCarthyesque nightmare for more moderate Mormons. Nevertheless, he never lost his ability to cast off criticism with humorous barbs. For instance, he remarked in 1952: "I am what the kindlier ones . . . would call a rabid reactionary (I am not, in fact, that). Some of the unkindly ones will shrug their shoulders and say, 'He is just a doddering old fogey.' I admit the age, but deny the rest of the allegation— the doddering and fogeyness. Some will join the issue with me on this personal estimate and conclusion; but so be it."[12]

In his later years, he joined often with fellow Mormon apostle Ezra Taft Benson (Eisenhower's secretary of agriculture and later church president) in expounding a Mormon brand of patriotism that tied inseparably "Americanism" and religious belief.[13] Clark's fire never went out, it just lost some of its light.[14]

On October 6, 1961, Joshua Reuben Clark, Jr., died in Salt Lake City at the age of ninety. The legacy he left was largely for his small community of Mormons who remembered his thirty years as "prophet, seer, and revelator," but for the nation as a whole he was a quickly forgotten figure. His reputation as international lawyer, diplomat, and as the prime mover in the work to salvage the defaulted foreign bonds of the depression, gained him little notice in history. Only his seventeen-page letter to the secretary of state in 1928, the now famous *Memorandum on the Monroe Doctrine*, accidentally provided a place for his name in the indexes of history books. His efforts to collect the foreign credits of countless Americans during the Great Depression, however, stand as a far better monument to Reuben Clark's role in the transition of America into the new order of the twentieth century. But as he would have said, "So be it."[15]

As for the Foreign Bondholders Protective Council, following Clark's retirement from the presidency, it continued to experience some of the same problems that Clark believed he had solved by the summer of 1938. Although criticism from domestic sources abated rapidly and the organization's hegemony in its field continued to solidify,[16] the world situation unavoidably began to work adversely upon the council's efforts. The Germans, for example, stepped up their attacks on the FBPC for refusing to accept the "reality of the present" and for continuing the immorality of the American financial establishment. "The fact is that the Americans were war profiteers," chided the Nazis, "and lacked all experience in the art of international finance, an art known before the war only to three countries, Britain, France, and Germany. The Council's reports are all in all merely admission of a mistaken American bank policy."[17] The Hitler regime thus told the world that the defaulted dollar bonds were the fault of the Americans themselves (certainly true to some extent), and hence the debtors had to feel no responsibility for the defaults.

In addition, the council's relationship with the government began another decline after its high point in May 1938 when Douglas and the SEC openly endorsed its integrity. This decline was due primarily to two factors. First, Francis White showed few of the same qualities of diplomatic wisdom that had graced Clark's dealings with Washington. Among his first acts as president, for example, was an ill-advised request for tax-exempt status for the council and its contributions. This involved the Departments of State and Treasury and the SEC in "a gritty problem" that enraptured no one.[18] He also evidently made some irritating mistakes that elicited a terse memorandum from Sumner Welles: "State Department has come to a point where if the Foreign Bondholders Protective Council continues to expect Department's help and active interest, they will have to abide by Department's recommendations as to policy. Suggests that Dr. Feis or Mr. Livesey should talk frankly to Mr. White concerning the situation."[19]

On the other hand, White's work in the negotiations field was admirable during his first year as president of the council, with successes coming particularly from Brazil and Costa Rica. Then, in the summer of 1939, the chaotic international scene suddenly seemed to break the fragile structure of building council successes. The Brazilians failed to resume debt service as they had promised, and Danzig, under the stress of the European war, reneged on its funding bond plan.[20] On top of all of this, the council had been unable to replace the portion of its financial base the 1938 reforms had eroded from it. Within a year, it sank into deep financial trouble, and White had to try such desperate moves as the tax exemption ploy and a request for the government to allow him to make the one-eighth percent donation mandatory in a resumption of service.[21] None of this was pleasing to an administration more concerned about a solid front against fascism than about the protection of the American holders of foreign securities.

The second element in the council's decline of favor in Washington had to do with the war in Europe and Roosevelt's scramble to "line up Latin America."[22] He instituted a campaign in late 1939 to gain the economic and political solidarity of the Western Hemisphere, and as one of his major enticements he offered a fresh extension of liberal American credits. Almost every Latin American state was, according to the council's reckoning, a defaulting debtor. Accordingly, on October 27, 1939, the president dealt the council a severe blow when he said that he desired "a more expeditious" adjustment of defaulted Latin American securities and announced himself in favor of scaling them down. This was something Clark and the council had refused to countenance. Roosevelt then added insult to injury by saying that he was rather disappointed in the work of the council, because it had "not gotten very far" in solving the Latin American debt problem.[23] A few days later, the White House received a letter of concordance from a citizen whose stinging remarks summarized the damage FDR's comment had done to the prestige of the council: "You can't expect anything else from an organization run by nice old women, such as I found in the office when I paid them a visit this Summer, and College Professors. I . . . really believe something can be done if the problem is approached from a practical standpoint rather than from the standpoint of an Economics College Professor or an old maid."[24]

Shortly after the president's statement, the administration announced that it was removing the council's authority to negotiate with the Latin Americans and was placing it directly with the State Department. Hans Morgenthau, a long-time critic, and the Colombian ambassador hailed the new negotiations formula in a joint attack upon the council. Morgenthau shrugged, "What has it done?" The ambassador added that he agreed "100%" with Roosevelt and Morgenthau, and that "it is very hard if you make a proposal after considerate study and you stand by that proposal, you are accused of presenting an ultimatum. Then, if you start low and work up, you are accused of trying to bargain like a peddler."[25]

Such was the harsh reward for the council's painstaking work to present the debtor nations with a firm American position. But rightly or wrongly, the expediency of foreign relations left the organization bereft of much of its raison d'etre, and it would shrink to practical inactivity during the war years. The council issued no reports during the war until 1944, when it came out with a lengthy summary of the foreign bond situation as it had evolved in the interim. Its 1945 *Annual Report* portended a renewal of activity: "The end of World War II would seem to call for many negotiations and adjustments of bond obligations. The notoriously wide-spread defaults of the early nineteen thirties were only partly remedied before the War precipitated new difficulties."[26]

Francis White left the presidency of the council, certainly disappointed, and James Grafton Rogers of Yale University assumed the mantle at the end of World War II. The council slowly resumed its full activities. Happily, its financial picture had improved greatly because of its much-reduced expenses and a tougher requirement for contributions upon settlement,[27] but the scope of its work would never again take on the dimensions that it had during the great prophesying of the depression years. Nevertheless, by 1962, almost all of the governments that had defaulted during the depression and the war had resumed service on their dollar bonds.[28] The council, through sheer doggedness, could claim credit for most of the readjustment plans, and it continued to work with the remaining few defaulting states. Its efforts, of course, dwindled in importance as the bulk of defaults diminished after the war and with a return to international economic stability.[29]

Since World War II, the existence of the World Bank and the International Monetary Fund has lightened the council's burdens considerably. In addition, debtor nations in 1956 began to enter into voluntary debt rescheduling arrangements at the so-called Paris Club (for credits from official institutions) and the London Club (for credits from commercial banks).[30] The FBPC nevertheless continued to function under a succession of distinguished and dedicated presidents (Clark, White, Rogers, Dana Munro, George D. Woods, and John R. Petty), watching over the interests of private investors and demanding the respect of the financial and business worlds. While it worked gallantly to hold high the banner of international credit responsibility, its detractors persisted; bondholders, government officials, and special interest groups continued to snipe at its deliberate ways. In the postwar period, a pesky irritant who had the interesting name of Karl Marks set up shop a few doors down Broad Street and assigned himself the permanent task of watchdog to the council. As if to get away from him, the organization moved in 1969 to 1775 Broadway, where it remained until the office closed on December 31, 1980. After that, the FBPC continued to operate out of the Brooklyn home of Alice M. Popp, whom White had hired in February of 1939 to assist A. Helen Wylie, council head of staff. In 1948, council officials "eased Wylie out, because she was a woman,"[31] and Popp became the entire staff of the organization. She had the title of secretarial assistant to the president in 1952 and secretarial assistant to the council in 1975. When the office closed, the records of the FBPC went into storage in a Flatbush Avenue warehouse to await transfer to the library at Columbia University.[32]

The story of the Foreign Bondholders Protective Council remains unfinished. It is still technically in operation and boasts a highly distinguished board of directors, from whose business offices whatever work it performs goes forth. Among its numerous postwar accomplishments, it trumpets the fact that "98% to 99% of the bonds subject to [Council] offers have been assented to the plans."[33] But the full-blown glory of the Clark years is only a fading memory. The great fight against the vision of an end to international economic responsibility it waged during those fearful years from 1933 to 1939 is long-since over. Yet that early period of council history remains a potent symbol of the refusal of nineteenth-century America to pass away without a struggle, or at least without a hope for resurrection.

10

And It Came to Pass: A Summary

So I prophesied as he commanded me,
and the breath came into them,
and they lived, and stood up on their feet,
an exceeding great army.

In the years following 1919, the United States responded to its international coming of age by moving rapidly into the role of a creditor nation. Within a decade, private American holdings in foreign bonds amounted to something between $7 and $8 billion. As was to be the case in the domestic junk bond scandal of the 1980s, many of them were issued under extremely dangerous circumstances—high interest rates, poor security, and often simple dishonesty and deceit on the part of the debtors and the American issue houses offering the securities to the public. It only followed that with a world economic disaster on the scale of the Great Depression a major portion of such bonds would fall into default. Accordingly, by 1932 somewhere near a third of the foreign dollar bonds afloat in the United States were in some stage of default.

Other, more experienced creditor nations such as Great Britain had established protective councils under government sanction and cooperation that could apply pressure and institute negotiations with debtors to assure the viability of foreign bonds in such a situation. Working with this model, the Hoover administration initiated efforts to set up an American protective organization on the pattern of the British council. Congress even legislated for such a quasi-official agency, but under the Roosevelt administration, officials at the State Department decided to encourage instead the organization of a private body that would avoid embroiling the government in the delicate business of negotiating on defaulted foreign securities. Consequently, in Washington in 1933, administration officials sponsored a series of meetings among carefully selected men, resulting in the establishment of the Foreign Bondholders Protective Council in December of that year.

The council's first project involved Brazil to which it sent one of its founding members, J. Reuben Clark, Jr. His success in that negotiation and the illness of the group's first president worked to bring Clark into the leadership of the council early in 1934. A former ambassador and undersecretary of state, he had years of experience in international law and foreign affairs. Believing in the adjustment of claims by negotiation, Clark looked for a way to serve on the battle-line against the apparent erosion of the old order that came with the economic chaos of depression. He quickly plunged into the work of the council, where his great vigor earned him a reputation as "hard-fisted" and "acquisitive and stubborn." Concomitantly, his accession to the council presidency had other results that undeniably charted the course of the group's labors throughout the decade. He imbued it with his own ideas about hard work, morality, independence, and economic responsibility among nations even in the face of disaster. This molding of the council into Clark's image, however, also resulted in many problems that he, in turn, spent much of his four and a half years in the presidency overcoming. The council repaid his long service by becoming a vehicle in which Reuben Clark, a champion of the old universe of the nineteenth century, rode through the trauma of the emergent new order. It became a firm place for him to take his stand against the changes that threatened to disrupt the mythic structures that sustained his realities.

Under Clark's leadership, the incipient council passed through four discernible stages that culminated in what he believed to be a considerable vindication of his efforts. During the first phase (roughly 1933-34), the organization sampled both success and failure as it strived with debtors. The success bode well for the future, and the failure taught the council's officers something about the difficulty of their task. More portentously, the council became increasingly dependent upon financial institutions for support.

In the second phase (1935), this dependence fed a rising tide of criticism that worked against Clark's ability to act forcefully in his negotiations. It also helped to widen a rift that had begun to develop between the council and the government. That delicate relationship had so deteriorated by the end of 1935 that the State Department often exhibited something akin to embarrassment whenever the council "problem" arose. As a result of such suspicion, and because of the swell of criticism against the council (and particularly its financial base), the Securities and Exchange Commission opened a full-scale investigation of the council that threatened to destroy it in favor of direct governmental activity in the foreign securities field. Clark met this challenge head-on, hoping to answer every legitimate criticism frankly and satisfactorily.

The third phase (1936) found the council striving to make as much negotiations progress as possible while awaiting the SEC's decision. Following Clark's lead, it also changed its mood from one of conciliation toward the debtors to a hard line that struck out at the various practices of the defaulting governments Clark adjudged to be immoral or beyond the sanction of reason and international law.

In the final phase (1937-38), the council received the approbation of the SEC upon its conformity to the commission's recommendations for reform of the organization's financial base. Clark then moved vigorously to remove the sources of all criticism. Believing that he had successfully done so, and that the council's effectiveness and hegemony in the business were secure, he resigned the presidency and took a largely ceremonial title as chair of the executive committee, where he remained until 1945.

During this entire period of intense effort in the council's New York offices, Clark also fought the coming of the new age on another front. As a high cleric in the hierarchy of the Mormon church, he spent many months in Salt Lake City working to buttress his "Saints" against the evils of the New Deal by establishing a new Mormon communitarianism. He became the prime mover in the creation of a Church Security Plan that sought to remove all Mormons from public relief rolls and to care for them under a system of church-operated welfare projects. To this end, Clark commuted between Utah and New York for nearly five years to combat what he believed to be the insidious forces of a destructive revolution against eternal social verities.

The meaning of Reuben Clark's prophesying upon the bones of the old order might find circumscription within three spheres. First, it was an attack upon those powers of disintegration that seemed to be crushing the very foundations of civilization—lawlessness and irresponsibility on personal and institutional levels, and the apparent discarding of the basic virtues that had sustained the cosmos for so long. Second, it was a clear manifestation of the call for a return to the lost sense of community, a plea for unity against the faceless and treacherous trend toward welfare statism. Finally, it represented a cry in the wilderness for a return to the traditional system of values—thrift, hard work, independence, and small-group responsibility for the well-being of the needy. In short, Reuben Clark prophesied upon bones he believed still capable of life. Only in the misty vision of such an Old Testament prophet could they rise again, a mighty army to defend the maxims of the ancient universe.

Epilogue

The saga of the foreign debt crisis continues, its present manifestations rendering the problems of the thirties as insignificant by comparison. Between 1970 and 1982, the foreign debt of the so-called less-developed countries (LDCs) rose from some $100 billion to more than $500 billion. Then oil prices crashed. In a dramatic upward spiral, the LDC foreign debt quickly shot up to $1.051 trillion by 1989. Most ominously, in 1984 the flow of capital reversed; $43 billion left the LDCs for developed nations in 1988 alone.[1]

Economists quickly analyzed the problem,[2] which just as quickly revealed itself to be similar to that of the twenties and thirties. Facing an increasing need to create an economic infrastructure for development (schools, roads, communications facilities, ports, warehouses, and many other apparent prerequisites to growth), after World War II developing nations looked to three sources of funding (beyond foreign aid): private saving, government saving, and foreign saving. Inasmuch as the first was always limited by poor economies and the second was almost always nonexistent, they turned to the vast pool of foreign capital. Until the 1970s, their borrowing abroad usually fell within a reasonable ratio between debt and gross national product. But LDCs grappled with a continually sticky demand. They must somehow manipulate the balance of payments to keep the costs of their debt from running past the value of their exports, the principal means of obtaining funds to service debt. Unfortunately, many were "left with only a thin cushion of international reserves to protect themselves against unforeseen shocks."[3]

Repeating what had happened during the thirties and the previous debt crises, disaster inevitably arrived as the international economy sharply reduced export volumes and/or reduced the prices of exports.[4] In the 1980s, the major commodity culprit was oil, with devastating effects upon the debt situation in countries like Mexico and Indonesia. Indeed, one economic historian declared that the entire current crisis "officially began on August 20, 1982, when Mexico announced suspension of principal payments on its foreign debt."[5] To complicate matters, many LDCs had become increasingly dependent upon private creditors during the 1970s, just as they had in the 1920s.[6] In order to attract short-term foreign capital, they raised rates to make portfolio investments more attractive, which only added to the debt burden when the crunch came.[7]

Shortly after taking office in 1989, the Bush administration began to signal a dramatic shift in official American policy with regard to the debt crisis. Treasury Secretary Nicholas Brady put forth a plan offering incentives for commercial banks to write off a portion of their massive holdings in Third World debt paper. At the same time, the United States and other developed nations would increase financial support for countries willing to undertake sound adjustment policies in the medium-term, with new lending programs for LDCs guaranteeing economic, environmental, and/ or other reforms.[8] This new approach would also include highly inflationary "debt-equity swaps" in which multinational firms would purchase paper at deep discounts then swap it for local currency at the debtor's central bank.[9]

But the Brady plan addressed only the commercial debt problem, and calls continued for a broader scheme for forgiving Third World debts, perhaps to follow the pattern set at the 1988 Toronto summit of major industrial nations: creditors could "choose from a menu of rescheduling options, including a significant forgiveness of the amount rescheduled, a reduction in the interest rate on the rescheduled amount, and an extension of the grace period and maturity."[10] Actually, the Toronto plan traced closely (minus the forgiveness clause) the outline of various designs Clark and the FBPC had used in their work to reinvigorate the defaulted bonds of the 1930s.

In June 1990, President Bush proposed to forgive billions of dollars in Latin American official debt and suggested the creation of a "hemisphere-wide free trade zone" to discourage protectionism. Observers hailed this "new approach" as "long-awaited" and touted "forward momentum" in the search for a feasible solution to the Third World debt crisis.[11]

Nevertheless, more than half a century removed from his great struggle, the old prophet, were he still alive, might issue forth a new jeremiad. In 1990, with no end in sight, Third World countries' foreign debt rose another 4.3 percent to a staggering $1.096 trillion.[12]

Notes

ABBREVIATIONS USED IN THE NOTES

ACR[year]   *Report of the [no.] Annual Conference of the Church of Jesus Christ of Latter-day Saints* (Salt Lake City: LDS Church, [year])

Baker MS   Newton D. Baker, Papers, Manuscript Division, Library of Congress

FBPC[box]   Foreign Bondholders Protective Council, Papers, Pioneer Business Records Center, Brooklyn, New York

FBPCAR[year]   *Foreign Bondholders Protective Council, Inc., Annual Report, [year]* (New York: The Council, [year])

FR[year]   U.S., Department of State, *Papers Relating to the Foreign Relations of the United States, [year]*, vol. 1: *General* (Washington, D.C.: Government Printing Office, 1947-53)

JHLDS   Journal History of the Church of Jesus Christ of Latter-day Saints, Historical Department of the Church, Salt Lake City

JRCP[box]   J. Reuben Clark, Jr., Papers, Harold B. Lee Library, Brigham Young University, Provo, Utah

RDS[year]   U.S., Department of State, *Register of the Department of State, January 1, [year]* (Washington, D.C.: Government Printing Office, [year])

R&FA   Edgar B. Nixon, ed., *Franklin D. Roosevelt and Foreign Affairs,* vol. 1 (Cambridge: The Belknap Press of Harvard University Press, 1969)

RG59   Numerical File, National Archives Building, General
                  Records of the Department of State, Record Group 59
S-ACR[year]   *Report of the [no.] Semi-Annual Conference of the Church
                  of Jesus Christ of Latter-day Saints* (Salt Lake City: LDS
                  Church, [year])
SEC5   U.S., Securities and Exchange Commission, *Report on
                  the Study and Investigation of the Work, Activities,
                  Personnel and Functions of Protective and Reorganiza-
                  tion Committees,* part 5: *Protective Committees and
                  Agencies for the Holders of Defaulting Foreign Govern-
                  mental Bonds* (Washington, D.C.: Government Printing
                  Office, 1937)

CHAPTER 1: THE END OF THE NINETEENTH CENTURY

1. Gilbert Seldes, *The Years of the Locust* (Boston: Little, Brown, 1933).
2. Editorial, *Washington Post,* Dec. 31, 1932, p. 6.
3. Editorial, *New York Times,* Jan. 1, 1933, sec. 4, p. 4.
4. Charles C. Alexander, *Nationalism in American Thought, 1930-1945* (Chicago: Rand McNally, 1969), p. 9.
5. *Washington Post,* Jan. 1, 1933, p. 3.
6. *New York American,* Dec. 19, 1933, p. 30.
7. *New York Times,* Jan. 1, 1933, p. 1.
8. *Washington Post,* Jan. 1, 1933, p. 1.
9. *New York Times,* Jan. 1, 1933, p. 21.
10. Ibid., Jan. 2, 1933, p. 26.
11. *Washington Post,* Jan. 1, 1933, p. 19.
12. Ibid., p. 1.
13. *New York Times,* Jan. 1, 1933, pp. 1, 9.
14. Ibid., sec. 4, p. 4.
15. Ibid.
16. Ibid., Jan. 2, 1933, p. 26.
17. U.S., President, *Report of the President's Research Committee on Social Trends* (Washington, D.C.: Government Printing Office, 1932), pp. 3-4.
18. *Washington Post,* Jan. 1, 1933, p. 2. One wag, obviously thinking of Hoover's sad rejection and Roosevelt's difficult task, prophesied that "a child born this year may be President—if he's unlucky." Ibid., p. 1.
19. *New York Times,* Jan. 1, 1933, p. 1.
20. *Washington Post,* Jan. 1, 1933, p. 1.
21. Alexander, *Nationalism,* p. 3.

22. *Washington Post,* Jan. 1, 1933, p. 9.

23. *New York Times,* Jan. 2, 1933, p. 26.

24. *Washington Post,* Jan. 1, 1933, p. 2. This whimsy was successful, strangely enough, as Terino had to redeem only $35 worth of its "money"; souvenier hunters absorbed the rest.

25. Ibid., p. 6. "How can Senator Dill obtain 3.2 per cent beer for testing purposes without violating the Volstead Act?" questioned the *Post.*

26. *New York Times,* Jan. 2, 1933, p. 20

27. Ibid., Jan. 1, 1933, sec. 4, p. 7.

28. Ibid.

29. Herbert Feis, *1933: Characters in Crisis* (Boston: Little, Brown, 1966), part 1.

30. *Washington Post,* Jan. 2, 1933, p. 12

31. Ibid., Dec. 31, 1932, p. 5.

32. W. E. Heltzel to Cordell Hull, Jan. 26, 1934, 800.51/915, RG59.

33. H. J. Becker to Roosevelt, June 4, 1934, 800.51/1061, RG59.

34. Mrs. G. P. Gullion to Roosevelt, Dec. 12, 1934, 800.51/1086, RG59.

35. For an interesting discussion of the sticky problems of contract theory in international finance, see Vincent P. Crawford, *International Lending, Long-Term Credit Relationships, and Dynamic Contract Theory,* Princeton Studies in International Finance, no. 59 (Princeton, N.J.: Princeton University Department of Economics, 1987).

CHAPTER 2: THE FOREIGN BOND SITUATION, 1933

1. John Foster Dulles, "The Securities Act and Foreign Lending," *Foreign Affairs* 12 (1933): 44-45. (Dulles was at the time serving as counsel to a large New York banking house.) During the nineteenth century, much of America's meager experience as a foreign lender had been in Mexico, with problems dating back to the Lincoln administration. See Edgar Turlington, *Mexico and Her Foreign Creditors* (New York: Columbia University Press, 1930). American holding of foreign bonds went from about $500 million in 1900 to nearly $14 billion in 1933. James H. Ronald, "National Organizations for the Protection of Holders of Foreign Bonds," *George Washington Law Review* 3 (May 1933): 413.

2. SEC5, pp. 4-6.

3. FBPCAR1934, p. 9. Missing was the set of checks common to the domestic bond situation. "One may accurately characterize the representatives of holders of foreign bonds as possessing extensive power, free from control or restraint." SEC5, p. 37.

4. FBPCAR1934, pp. 102-217 passim; SEC5, p. 6. See also Ilse S.

Mintz, *Deterioration of the Quality of Foreign Bonds Issues in the United States, 1920-1930* (New York: Arno Press, 1978); Barry J. Eichengreen and Peter H. Lindert, eds., *The International Debt Crisis in Historical Perspective* (Cambridge, Mass.: MIT Press, 1989).

5. FBPCAR1934, p. 12.

6. Ezekiel 37:1-10.

7. For evidence of the "small" nature of the average foreign investment, see FBPCAR1935, p. 99.

8. FBPCAR1934, pp. 102-217, passim.

9. Dulles, "Securities Act," p. 40.

10. SEC5, pp. 6-7.

11. Peter H. Lindert and Peter J. Morton, "How Sovereign Debt Has Worked," in *Developing Country Debt and the World Economy,* ed. Jeffrey D. Sachs (Chicago: University of Chicago Press, 1989), p. 226.

12. John H. Makin, *The Global Debt Crisis: America's Growing Involvement* (New York: Basic Books, 1984), p. 36. Makin presents a very readable history of eight centuries of governmental borrowing and repudiations while making cogent comparisons between the lending waves of the 1920s and 1970s and the crises of the 1930s and 1980s. "It is chastening to reflect, that after fifty years' experience, the function of an international lender of last resort is less well developed in the 1980s for the international financial system than it was for the United States during the early 1930s" (p. 26).

13. SEC5, p. 18. Generally, the overly appraised security clauses received (to the exclusion of other offsetting factors) additional publicity in investment books of reference and manuals, and thence in the press. Even so, more often than not the draftsmanship of foreign bond issues was so inadequate as to conceal defects, if not to produce them, in and of itself.

14. SEC5, p. 8.

15. Ibid., p. 9.

16. Philip A. Wellons, *Passing the Buck: Banks, Governments and Third World Debt* (Boston: Harvard Business School Press, 1987).

17. John T. Madden, Marcus Nadler, and Harry C. Sauvain, *America's Experience as a Creditor Nation* (New York: Prentice, 1937), pp. 206-31.

18. U.S., Congress, Senate, Committee on Banking and Currency, *Report of the Committee on Banking and Currency on Stock Exchange Practices,* S. Rept. 1455, 73rd Cong., 2d sess., 1934, p. 125.

19. Ibid., p. 126.

20. SEC5, p. 19.

21. Ibid.

22. Ibid., p. 22, quoting Allen W. Dulles.

23. FBPCAR1935, pp. 122-26; FBPCAR1936, p. 572; FBPCAR1937, pp. 459-66.

24. Feis, *1933,* pp. 267-68.

25. SEC5, p. 21.

26. Ibid., p. 10.

27. Quoted in Ralph Reisner, "Default by Foreign Sovereign Debtors: An Introductory Perspective," *University of Illinois Law Review* 1 (1982): 20.

28. Summary of the Institute of International Finance Annual Report, 1933, 800.51/907, RG59; see also *Commercial and Financial Chronicle,* Nov. 18, 1933, pp. 3618-19. "Since the abandonment of the gold standard by the United States and the revocation of the gold clause contracts, a number of foreign borrowers have also disregarded the gold clause in their obligations and have paid their debt service in depreciated dollars—a technical default."

29. SEC5, pp. 29-30.

30. Fred L. Block, *The Origins of International Economic Disorder: A Study of United States International Monetary Policy from World War II to the Present* (Berkeley: University of California Press, 1977), pp. 12-31. An associate of Joyce and Gabriel Kolko and William Appleman Williams, Block took the New Left view of the lending wave, arguing that the United States had the capacity to stabilize the world economy but did not do so because of essentially neoimperialist conflicts of interest.

31. Joan Hoff Wilson, *American Business and Foreign Policy, 1920-1933* (Boston: Beacon, 1973), ch. 4.

32. Barry Eichengreen, "The U.S. Capital Market and Foreign Lending," in *Developing Country Debt,* ed. Sachs, p. 240. See also Eichengreen and Richard Portes, "Debt and Default in the 1930s: Causes and Consequences," *European Economic Review* 30 (June 1986): 559-640, published first as Discussion Paper 1186 by the Harvard Institute of Economic Research.

33. Joseph S. Davis, *The World Between Wars—1919-39: An Economist's View* (Baltimore: Johns Hopkins University Press, 1975), p. 148.

34. Makin, *Global Debt Crisis,* p. 46. See also Arminio Fraga, *German Reparations and the Brazilian Debt: A Comparative Study,* Essays in International Finance, no. 163 (Princeton: N.J.: Princeton University Department of Economics, 1986), pp. 2-7, an excellent review of the German experience, 1919-31; Derek H. Aldcroft, *From Versailles to Wall Street, 1919-1929* (Berkeley: University of California Press, 1977), a good analysis of the origins of the German debt problem; T. Balderston, "The Beginnings of the Depression in Germany, 1927-30: Investment and the Capital Market," *Economic History Review* 35 (Aug. 1983): 395-415; Stephen A. Schuker, *American "Reparations" to Germany, 1919-33: Implications for the Third World Debt Crisis,* Princeton Studies in International Finance, no. 61 (Princeton, N.J.: Princeton University Department of Economics, 1988).

35. Makin, *Global Debt Crisis,* p. 50.

36. Ibid., pp. 46-49.

37. J. C. Sanchez Arnau, "Debt and Development," in *Debt and Development*, ed. J. C. Sanchez Arnau (New York: Praeger, 1982), p. 5. Sanchez Arnau's collection of essays rotates around the notions of dependency theory, developed by the Nobel Prize-winning economist Gunnar Myrdal and refined by the American economist Paul Baran and others. Peter Evans, *Dependent Development: The Alliance of Multinational, State, and Local Capital in Brazil* (Princeton, N.J.: Princeton University Press, 1979), pp. 25-27, credits the theory's founding to Latin American sociologists and historians, among them Caio Prado, Jr., Sergio Bagu, F. H. Cardozo, T. dos Santos, and Florestan Fernandes. The essential argument of dependency theorists is, in the words of Baran, "that the main interest of foreign investors lay in freezing the international division of labor so that the less developed countries continued to be producers of raw materials." Ibid., p. 19. See also J. Samuel Valenzuela and Arturo Valenzuela, "Modernization and Dependency: Alternative Perspectives in the Study of Latin American Underdevelopment," *Comparative Politics* 10 (July 1978): 535-57.

38. Carlos Marichal, *A Century of Debt Crises in Latin America: From Independence to the Great Depression, 1820-1930* (Princeton, N.J.: Princeton University Press, 1989). Marichal represents a generation of Latin American scholars who seek to revise the history of debt crises from the point of view of the debtors and with an eye toward shifting the blame away from debtor malfeasance. While recognizing the validity of much of Marichal's argument, David Felix, reviewing his book in the *Journal of Economic History* 49 (Dec. 1989): 1037-38, faults him for "underemphasizing" certain "complicatory Latin American behavior" and "passing lightly over" other debtor errors in order to exculpate leaders among borrowing nations at the expense of the lenders. For a representative country-specific example, see J. Manuel Uriarte, *Transnational Banks and the Dynamics of Peruvian Foreign Debt and Inflation* (New York: Praeger, 1985).

39. Georges Corm, "The Indebtedness of the Developing Countries: Origins and Mechanisms," in *Debt and Development*, ed. Sanchez Arnau, p. 79. While presenting a good history of the innerworkings of external debt in the third world, particularly from 1814 to 1914, Corm curiously glosses over the interwar period.

40. Albert Fishlow, "Coping with the Creeping Crisis of Debt," in *Politics and Economics of External Debt Crisis: The Latin American Experience,* ed. Miguel S. Wionczek and Luciano Tomassini (Boulder: Westview Press, 1985), p. 138.

41. Makin, *Global Debt Crisis*, p. 44. Finding the similarities between the lending explosions of the 1920s and 1970s "remarkable," Makin cites the same intensity with which bankers in both eras pushed the loans and the

similitude of the stamps of approval issued by the League of Nations and the IMF. Robert Henriques Girling, *Multinational Institutions and the Third World: Management, Debt, and Trade Conflicts in the International Economic Order* (New York: Praeger, 1985), presents another useful albeit cursory comparison of the two eras. Still another is Marc Janssens De Grauwe and Hilde Leliaert, *Real-Exchange-Rate Variability from 1920 to 1926 and 1973-1982,* Princeton Studies in International Finance, no. 56 (Princeton, N.J.: Princeton University Department of Economics, 1985). On the other hand, Angus Maddison, *Two Crises: Latin America and Asia, 1929-39 and 1973-83* (Washington, D.C.: Organization for Economic Cooperation and Development, 1985), emphasizes considerable differences. Lindert and Morton, "Sovereign Debt," p. 227, note that bond dealing had been the rule in international lending until the bank-loan wave of 1974-82.

42. SEC5, p. 10.

43. Ibid, p. 36.

44. Ibid., pp. 10-12.

45. Edwin M. Borchard, *The Diplomatic Protection of Citizens Abroad* (New York: Academy of Political and Social Science, 1928), pp. 305-7.

46. SEC5, pp. 13-16. Some bondholders' representatives, however, did believe that suits were useful in bringing publicity to a default situation. *New York Times,* April 26, 1936, p. 28.

47. Borchard, *Diplomatic Protection,* pp. 305-7.

48. Feis, *1933,* p. 268.

49. F. J. Lisman, "Protective Committees for Security Holders," *Harvard Business Review* 13 (1934): 20; SEC5, pp. 119-20.

50. SEC5, p. 10. Even so, until 1933 bankers dominated completely efforts at readjustment.

51. Ibid., pp. 23-25.

52. Luis Maria Drago, "State Loans in Their Relation to International Policy," in *The Monroe Doctrine: Its Importance in the International Life of the States of the New World,* ed. Alejandro Alvarez (New York: Oxford University Press, 1924), pp. 244-57.

53. James Brown Scott, ed., *The Hague Conventions and Declarations of 1899 and 1907* (New York: Carnegie Endowment for International Peace, 1915), pp. 89-95.

54. SEC5, p. 27.

55. Ibid., p. 28; Ronald, "National Organizations," p. 412: "A myriad of delicate problems in international relations arise as soon as citizens of one country invest in bonds of another country, be they direct or portfolio investments. The problems of intervention, of recognition, of pledged revenues, of international financial supervision, of concessions for economic enterprise, of governmental control of stock exchange listing, of governmen-

tal prohibition of the dealing in bonds of defaulting foreign countries, of foreign office 'censorship' of proposed flotations—all may become highly inflammatory phases of international relations."

56. Franklin D. Roosevelt, *The Year of Crisis, 1933*, vol. 2 of *The Public Papers and Addresses of Franklin D. Roosevelt*, ed. S. I. Rosenman, 13 vols. (New York: Random House, 1938-50), pp. 413-14.

57. Feis, *1933*, p. 268.

58. Ronald, "National Organizations," p. 411; FBPCAR1934, pp. 13-14.

59. The British Council of Foreign Bondholders came into being in 1869. Belgian and French counterparts organized in 1898. See Ronald, "National Organizations," pp. 428-31.

60. Feis, *1933*, p. 266; see also Feis, *Europe, the World's Banker, 1870-1914* (New Haven: Yale University Press, 1930). A Harvard-trained economist, Feis served as advisor to the Department of State for international economic affairs from 1931 to 1943.

Chapter 3: Divining the Miracle

1. U.S., Congress, Senate, *Department of State Rule of March 3, 1922*, Sen. Doc. 187, 71st Cong., 2d sess., 1930.

2. Ronald, "National Organizations," pp. 438-39, 443.

3. U.S., Congress, Senate, S. Res. 305, 71st Cong., 3d sess., Feb. 26, 1931, *Congressional Record*, p. 6103.

4. Charles Cheney Hyde, "The Department of State on the American Flotation for Foreign Public Loans," *American Journal of International Law* 16 (1922): 251-54. Hyde served as an editor of the *Journal*.

5. Feis, *1933*, p. 268.

6. Ibid., p. 269. The two realized from the beginning that the many problems incident to the formation of such a group would make the process a lengthy one.

7. SEC5, pp. 35-36.

8. Ibid., p. 35.

9. *The Times* (London), Nov. 22, 1918, p. 32.

10. Ronald, "National Organizations," p. 443.

11. *New York Times*, Oct. 2, 1931, p. 31.

12. SEC5, pp. 48-51, 53.

13. Winkler published a book, *Foreign Bonds, An Autopsy: A Study of Defaults and Repudiations of Government Obligations* (Philadelphia: Roland Swain, 1933), a sometimes nonsensical survey of the causes of the default phenomenon. It laid little blame on anyone, but it had nothing bad to

say about brokers specifically. Winkler undoubtedly wrote the book to get in on the ground floor of a coming government-sponsored corporation.

14. *New York Times,* March 6, 1932, p. 30.

15. SEC5, pp. 53-58.

16. Ibid., pp. 99-101.

17. Ibid., p. 100.

18. Ibid., pp. 102-3, 111.

19. Feis, *1933,* p. 269.

20. SEC5, pp. 62-63. FBPCAR1934, p. 9, reported erroneously that "the movement progressed no farther than this initial meeting."

21. U.S., Department of State, *Press Release,* April 16, 1932, p. 362; *New York Times,* April 16, 1932, p. 31; Ronald, "National Organizations," p. 447.

22. SEC5, p. 66.

23. SEC5, pp. 63-65; Feis, *1933,* p. 269.

24. Ronald, "National Organizations," p. 447.

25. Feis, *1933,* p. 269.

26. SEC5, p. 65. Bankers were not to be members of the council, however.

27. Feis, *1933,* p. 270.

28. Ibid.

29. The organization committee continued to function nevertheless. See FR1933, p. 935.

30. See particularly Stimson writing in *Commerce and Finance Chronicle* 134 (1932): 209.

31. *New York Times,* Aug. 11, 1932, p. 1.

32. Ibid., Aug. 12, 1932, p. 1.

33. Ronald, "National Organizations," pp. 440-42. During the New Deal, the administration adopted this as policy in their comments on foreign securities. It was really no better than the old policy, for if the government remained silent on an issue, then the public assumed it to be good.

34. Feis, *1933,* pp. 270-71.

35. Ibid., p. 270.

36. U.S., Congress, Senate, 73d Cong., 1st sess., May 8, 1933, *Congressional Record,* 77, pp. 1987-89.

37. Ronald, "National Organizations," p. 445; also correspondence concerning Title II in the Roosevelt Library printed in R&FA, pp. 115-17, 152, 334-36, 338.

38. FR1933, pp. 934-36; see also Feis, *1933,* p. 272.

39. FR1933, p. 936.

40. Ibid. Certainly the frenzy of the "100 days" pushed the foreign bond problem into the background of the administration's concerns. See also

SEC5, pp. 69-70; Feis, *1933,* pp. 273-74.

41. Ronald, "National Organizations," p. 448.

42. Feis, *1933,* p. 273. See also Roosevelt, *Public Papers,* 2:414; Roosevelt to Rayburn, May 20, 1933, OF 242:T, R&FA, p. 152; Roosevelt to Johnson, July 31, 1933, OF 100-B:CT, R&FA, p. 338.

43. Ronald, "National Organizations," pp. 446-47.

44. Lisman, "Protective Committees," pp. 19-20; see also Feis to Hull, May 10, 1933, OF 100-B:CT, R&FA, pp. 115-16.

45. Richard Washburn Child to Roosevelt, May 11, 1933, OF 242:T5, R&FA, pp. 116-17; Child to Roosevelt, May 25, 1933, Roosevelt Papers, cited in Feis, *1933,* pp. 174-275.

46. Roosevelt, *Public Papers,* 2:414. The president seemed to enjoy equivocating about the debt issue in general. See, for example, ibid., p. 174.

47. SEC5, pp. 67-68.

48. SEC5, pp. 51-53, 57-60.

49. Feis, *1933,* p. 275.

50. *New York Times,* June 4, 1933, sec. 2, p. 5.

51. Ibid., July 25, 1933, p. 27.

52. Stevens to Roosevelt, July 28, 1933, OF 100-B:TS, R&FA, pp. 334-36. See also Stevens to Roosevelt, Aug. 5, 1933, ibid., pp. 348-49.

53. Ibid., Aug. 4, 1933, p. 2.

54. Ibid., Oct. 8, 1933, sec 2, p. 9.

55. Roosevelt to Hull, Morgenthau, and Roper (secretary of commerce), Aug. 31, 1933, OF 100-B:CT, R&FA, p. 382.

56. Feis, *1933,* pp. 275-76. Feis felt snubbed when he was not invited to this meeting, an experience that left him "smarting" and undoubtedly embittered toward the council. It may also help to account for the many (mostly minor) differences between the Feis account of the birth of the FBPC and those of the council itself and the Securities and Exchange Commission.

57. *New York Times,* Oct. 8, 1933, sec. 2, p. 9; Oct. 18, 1933, p. 31; Oct. 19, 1933, p.5.

58. Feis, *1933,* p. 276.

59. Ibid., quoting Stimson Diary, Oct. 26, 1933; see also Johnson to Roosevelt, Aug. 26, 1933, OF 100-B:TC, R&FA, pp. 377-81.

60. FBPCAR1934, pp. 9-10. This form of invitation was Stevens's idea. Stevens to Roosevelt, Oct. 5, 1933, OF 100-B:TC, R&FA, pp. 417-18.

61. FBPCAR1934, pp. 10-11. Those attending the conference were Stevens; Laird Bell, a Chicago lawyer; Hendon Chubb of Chubb and Son (Marine Insurance), New York; W. L. Clayton, a Houston cotton dealer; John Cowles, a Des Moines publisher; Herman Ekern, former attorney general of Wisconsin; Ernest M. Hopkins, president of Dartmouth College; Philip LaFollette, former governor of Wisconsin; Mills B. Lane, a Georgia

banker; Frank O. Lowden, former governor of Illinois; Orrin K. McMurray, dean of the Law School, University of California; Roland S. Morris, former ambassador to Japan; Thomas D. Thacher, former solicitor-general; John C. Traphagen, New York banker; and Quincy Wright, professor of international law, University of Chicago. See also Ronald, "National Organizations," p. 448.

62. FBPCAR1934, pp. 9-10.

63. *New York Times,* Oct. 21, 1933, pp. 21, 25; Oct. 23, 1933, p. 14. It was true that Hull had made clear his opposition to Title II. See, for example, ibid., Oct. 19, 1933, p. 5. Still, Roosevelt made up his mind against Title II before it ever passed in the Congress.

64. Roosevelt, *Public Papers,* 2:411-13; FBPCAR1934, pp. 10-13; SEC5, pp. 76, 632-722, passim.

Chapter 4: Anointing the Prophet

1. The heart of the so-called First New Deal, the NIRA represented a genuine flirtation with national socialism. Although some historians argue that the Second New Deal (after the Supreme Court declared NIRA unconstitutional) was more radical, it enthroned old ideas of competition and mere protection of business.

2. FBPCAR1934, pp. 26-27; 832.51/800s, RG59.

3. *New York Times,* Oct. 24, 1933, p. 12. Also to be in the American delegation were Sophonisba Breckenridge, Alexander W. Weddell, Hull, J. Butler Wright, and Spruille Braden. See photograph in ibid., Dec. 17, 1933, p. 8.

4. FBPCAR1934, p. 27; Summary of the Work of J. Reuben Clark, Jr., in Rio de Janeiro, Dec., 1933-Jan., 1934, 832.51/800s, RG59. See also Frank W. Fox, *J. Reuben Clark, the Public Years* (Provo, Utah: Brigham Young University Press, 1980), pp. 590-94.

5. Ronald, "National Organizations," p. 449, sees the delay as solely the result of Stevens's illness.

6. Bell to Feis, Oct. 31, 1933, 800.51/935, RG59. Bell would soon receive baptism by fire.

7. Paris legation to Feis, Nov. 16, 1933, 800.51/881, RG59. Functioning councils similar to the proposed American organization existed in Britain (1869), Belgium (1898), France (1898), Switzerland (1919), Germany (1927), and the Netherlands (1930). See Ronald, "National Organizations," pp. 412-35.

8. Paris legation to Feis, Nov. 9, 1933, 800.51/886, RG59; Box 98, Baker MS.

9. *New York Times,* Oct. 19, 1933, p. 5.

10. Hull to Department of State, telegram, Nov. 28, 1933, 800.51/888, RG59.

11. Department of State to Hull, telegram, Nov. 28, 1933, 800.51/891, RG59.

12. SEC5, p. 85.

13. Department of State to Hull, telegram, Dec. 7, 1933, 800.51/897a, RG59.

14. 800.51/896, RG59. After the council's organization on December 18, Lavis wrote to the executive committee expressing the hope "that I might have some voice in the conduct of its Latin American affairs."

15. SEC5, pp. 51-53, 61-62.

16. Ibid., p. 77.

17. FBPCAR1934, pp. 13-25.

18. See *New York Times,* Dec. 19, 1933, p. 35, for the FBPC press statement following the conference.

19. SEC5, p. 79.

20. Ibid., pp. 78-81. Stevens was to receive $20,000 per annum; see also FBPCAR1935, p. 535.

21. FBPCAR1934, pp. 17-18. See also Feis, *1933,* p. 276; FR1933, pp. 937-39; *Washington Post,* Dec. 19, 1933, p. 3. For the *New York American,* Dec. 19, 1933, the FBPC founding did not even deserve a notation. The Hearst paper was more impressed with the landing on the Hudson River of Charles Lindbergh in a water plane. "Whenever you see him zooming down, you get a thrill that would nickle-plate a baked apple." Ibid., p. 30.

22. *New York Times,* Jan. 7, 1934, sec. 2, p. 7; Dec. 20, 1933, p. 20; Dec. 22, 1933, p. 25.

23. FBPCAR1934, pp. 28-29.

24. Ibid., p. 29.

25. Ibid., pp. 29, 36-43. The differences in the Niemeyer plan and the Brazilian decree are extremely subtle.

26. *New York Times,* Jan. 7, 1934, sec. 2, p. 7; Jan. 24, 1934, p. 27. For a contemporary analysis of the German situation, see C. R. S. Harris, *Germany's Foreign Indebtedness* (London: Oxford University Press, 1935).

27. Minutes of the Executive Committee, Feb. 14, 1934, FBPC45.

28. *Deseret News* (Salt Lake City), Feb. 16, 1934, p. 3. Clark subsequently reported to the State Department in Washington, *New York Times,* Feb. 25, 1934, sec. 2, p. 7.

29. Minutes of the Executive Committee, Feb. 26, 1934, FBPC45. The committee granted Stevens a subsistence allowance of $500 per month and Clark a salary of $20,000 per year plus travel and living expenses for services as acting president and chair of the executive committee.

30. FBPCAR1934, pp. 25-26.

31. Leonard J. Arrington and Davis Bitton, *The Mormon Experience: A History of the Latter-day Saints* (New York: Alfred A. Knopf, 1979), p. 291; Joseph Fielding Smith, *Essentials in Church History* 18th ed. (Salt Lake City: Deseret Book Company, 1963), pp. 644, 691-92. The Mormons wanted Clark in the First Presidency so badly that they kept the vacancy open for him for more than a year while he finished his work in Mexico. Smith, *Church History*, p. 645. For a complete account of Clark's church career, see D. Michael Quinn, *J. Reuben Clark, the Church Years* (Provo, Utah: Brigham University Press, 1983), in particular on his calling to the First Presidency, pp. 35-44.

32. J. Reuben Clark, Jr., *Immortality and Eternal Life* (Salt Lake City: Deseret News Press, 1969), 2:74.

33. Fox, *Clark*, pp. 594-95.

34. Clark nevertheless agreed to accept $400 a month for travel. Inasmuch as this brought his pay to an effective $19,800, critics would later see the salary cut as largely ceremonial. SEC5, pp. 79-80.

35. Quoted in SEC5, p. 83.

36. Feis, *1933*, p. 267.

37. J. Reuben Clark, Jr., "The Oil Settlement with Mexico," *Foreign Affairs* 6 (1928): 600-614; Clark, *The Petroleum Controversy in Mexico* (Salt Lake City: Deseret News Press, 1936).

38. J. Reuben Clark, "Jurisdiction of American-British Claims Commission," *American Journal of International Law* 7 (Oct. 1913): 707. See also Clark, "The Pacific Settlement of International Disputes," *Unity* 92 (Oct. 1923): 35-48.

39. Quoted in L. Ethan Ellis, *Frank B. Kellogg and American Foreign Relations* (New Brunswick: Rutgers University Press, 1961), p. 50.

40. Marion G. Romney, "J. Reuben Clark, Jr.: An Appreciation," paper presented at the J. Reuben Clark, Jr., Symposium, Brigham Young University, Provo, Utah, Nov. 23, 1972.

41. Max Weber, *The Protestant Ethic and the Spirit of Capitalism*, trans. Talcott Parsons (New York: Charles Scribner's Sons, 1958). pp. 180ff.

42. See *The Doctrine and Covenants of the Church of Jesus Christ of Latter-day Saints* (Salt Lake City: LDS Church, 1956), pp. 141, 163, 190, 215-16.

43. Ibid., p. 63.

44. J. Reuben Clark, Jr., *Education: A World Challenge to Parents and Teachers* (Salt Lake City: Deseret News Press, 1938), p. 2.

45. Weber, *Protestant Ethic*, p. 17.

46. J. Reuben Clark, Jr., *Work, Work Always* (Provo, Utah: Brigham Young University Press, 1960), p. 4.

47. *New York Times,* Feb. 27, 1934, p. 31.

CHAPTER 5: A REALLY HARD-FISTED MORMON

1. Feis, *1933,* p. 267.
2. Roosevelt demonstrated no consternation at his March 9 news conference over Clark's accession. R&FA, 2:21.
3. In "Isolationists of the 1930s and 1940s: A Historiographical Essay," a paper presented at the Southeastern Regional Meeting of the Society for Historians of American Foreign Relations, Feb. 24, 1973, p. 27, Justus D. Doenecke called for a biography of J. Reuben Clark to fill a void in the post-presidential years of Herbert Hoover as part of needed research on Republican isolationism. In the early 1970s, scholars at Mormon-owned Brigham Young University began a multivolume biography of Clark, mining the vast collection of his papers on deposit in the school's special collections. David H. Yarn, Jr., a philosopher, initially had exclusive access to the papers and produced *Young Reuben: The Early Life of J. Reuben Clark, Jr.* (Provo, Utah: Brigham Young University Press, 1974), and "Biographical Sketch of J. Reuben Clark, Jr.," *BYU Studies* 13 (Spring 1973): 5-14. Subsequently, two BYU history professors assumed the significant responsibility for the project and produced major works on Clark's life, non-Mormon Frank Fox on his public career and Mormon Michael Quinn on his church service. Fox's book (1980) answers Doenecke's challenge and stands as an exceptional achievement in excellent biography, despite the constraints under which he labored. Church rules, for example, would not allow Fox to refer to the "general authority" by his last name only, forcing the awkward use of Clark's first name and various titles throughout the work. While certainly adequate and often surprisingly candid, the Quinn volume (1983) is less admirable, relying heavily on church sources and suffering from a parochial view that taints its insights. For his part, Yarn continued to serve as "general editor" of the series and oversaw the collection of three volumes of *Selected Papers* (Provo, Utah: Brigham Young University Press), the first "On Religion, Education, and Youth" (1984), a second "On International Affairs" (1987), and finally "On Americanism and National Affairs" (1987).
4. Diaries and Records of Joshua Reuben Clark and Mary Louisa Woolley Clark, typescript, Special Collections, Brigham Young University Library, Provo, Utah, 1:400ff.
5. See, for example, James E. Talmage, "The Earth and Man," *The Instructor,* Dec., 1965, pp. 474-77, Jan., 1966, pp. 9-11, 15. Talmage originally delivered this address in the Salt Lake Tabernacle, Aug. 9, 1931.
6. Fox, *Clark,* p. 15.

7. Yarn, "Clark," p. 6.

8. See his own comments on his career in J. Reuben Clark, Jr., "The Charted Course of the Church in Education," speech delivered at Aspen Grove, Utah, Aug., 1938, Special Collections, Brigham Young University, Provo, Utah.

9. George D. Parkinson, "How a Utah Boy Won His Way," *Improvement Era,* March 1914, pp. 558ff.

10. Yarn, "Clark," p. 7.

11. RDS1929, p. 122.

12. Parkinson, "Utah Boy," p. 564; see also Ellis, *Kellogg,* p. 50.

13. *New York Times,* Aug. 18, 1928, p. 8; Fox, *Clark,* pp. 71-86.

14. Parkinson, "Utah Boy," p. 560; *Proceedings of the American Society of International Law* (1962), 70.

15. J. Reuben Clark, Jr., "Political Offenders and Offenses in Extradition," *American Journal of International Law* 3 (1909): 459.

16. The most important of these was the Alsop case in which the United States received a large award under British arbitration from Chile. See U.S., Department of State, Office of the Solicitor, *Distribution of the Alsop Award by the Secretary of State* (Washington, D.C.: Government Printing Office, 1912); FR1911, pp. 38-53. The Chileans felt coerced, and the relations between Chile and the United States took a turn for the worse. See William Roderick Sherman, *The Diplomatic and Commercial Relations of the United States and Chile, 1820-1914* (Boston: Badger, 1926), pp. 203-8; Parkinson, "Utah Boy," p. 562.

17. U.S., Department of State, Office of the Solicitor, *Right to Protect Citizens in Foreign Countries by Landing Forces* (Washington, D.C.: Government Printing Office, 1934); *New York Times,* Oct. 28, 1928, sec. 10, p. 13.

18. Edwin B. Firmage and Christopher Blakesley, "J. Reuben Clark, Jr.: Law and International Order," *BYU Studies* 13 (Spring 1973): 47.

19. See Fox, *Clark,* pp. 87-235, for a detailed accounting of Clark's service in Taft's State Department.

20. Firmage and Blakesley, "International Order," p. 48.

21. Ibid.; *New York Times,* Oct. 28, 1928, sec. 10, p. 13; Aug. 18, 1928, p. 8; Fox, *Clark,* pp. 235-72.

22. U.S., Department of Justice, *Emergency Legislation,* ed. J. Reuben Clark, Jr. (Washington, D.C.: Government Printing Office, 1918); *New York Times,* Oct. 28, 1928, sec. 10, p. 13.

23. Fox, *Clark,* pp. 271-72.

24. U.S., Department of State, *Data on the German Peace Treaty* (Washington, D.C.: Government Printing Office, 1919); also printed as Sen. Doc. 86, 66th Cong., 1st sess., 1919.

25. J. Reuben Clark, Jr., "Permanent Court of International Justice of the League of Nations," unpublished memorandum, May 28, 1923, Special Collections, Brigham Young University Library, Provo, Utah.

26. *New York Times,* Oct. 28, 1928, sec. 10, p. 13. See also Fox, *Clark,* pp. 273-98.

27. Yarn, "Clark," p. 9.

28. See Fox, *Clark,* pp. 299-336, for an excellent chronicle of Clark's service under Hughes.

29. RDS1929, p. 122; see also A. H. Feller, *The Mexican Claims Commission (1923-1934): A Study in the Law and Procedure of International Tribunals* (New York, 1935), pp. 284-89. See Fox, *Clark,* pp. 339-446, for a wonderfully analytical view of Clark's life between 1913 and 1926.

30. *New York Times,* Aug. 18, 1928, p. 8; Howard F. Cline, *The United States and Mexico* (Cambridge: Harvard University Press, 1953), pp. 128-212, passim; Wendell C. Gordon, *The Expropriation of Foreign-Owned Property in Mexico* (Washington, D.C.: American Council on Public Affairs, 1941), pp. 43ff; Ellis, *Kellogg,* p. 47; Clark, "Oil Settlement," pp. 600-614.

31. RDS1929, p. 6.

32. Ellis, *Kellogg,* p. 11.

33. *New York Times,* Aug. 18, 1928, p. 8. Ellis, *Kellogg,* p. 11, intimated that this somewhat tardy appointment came about simply because Kellogg found few good candidates. Graham H. Stuart, *The Department of State: A History of Its Organization, Procedure, and Personnel* (New York: Macmillan, 1949), p. 291, noted the following about the Clark appointment: "At first it was expected that a career man would be chosen, but President Coolidge, after delaying six weeks, named an eminent international lawyer, J. Reuben Clark, Jr. His background and experience and proven ability made his appointment a highly commendable one." See Fox, *Clark,* pp. 449-502, for a detailed history of Clark's diplomatic career before his appointment as undersecretary.

34. Clark received a recess commission on August 17 and entered duty on August 31. RDS1930, p. 6; RDS1934, p. 298. He was nominated on December 4 and confirmed on January 23, 1929. *Executive Journal* 77:54, 327.

35. *New York Times,* Aug, 18, 1928, p. 8; American Consul at Chihuahua to Kellogg, Sept. 5, 1928, 11.16/94, RG59.

36. Robert H. Ferrell, *Peace in Their Time: The Origins of the Kellogg-Briand Pact* (New Haven: Yale University Press, 1952).

37. See Kellogg's correspondence with Senator William Borah on the subject, Papers of William Edgar Borah, Box 542, Manuscript Division, Library of Congress.

38. *New York Times,* March 12, 1929, p. 3.

39. Ellis, *Kellogg,* p. 102.

40. U.S., Department of State, *Memorandum on the Monroe Doctrine* (Washington, D.C.: Government Printing Office, 1930). Kellogg prepared a policy statement based upon the Clark treatise, but the State Department never saw fit to release it. FR1929, 1:698-719.

41. Gene A. Sessions, "The Clark Memorandum Myth," *The Americas* 34 (July 1977): 40-58; Robert H. Ferrell, "Repudiation of a Repudiation," *Journal of American History* 51 (March 1965): 669-73.

42. Lee H. Burke, "J. Reuben Clark, Jr.: Under Secretary of State," *BYU Studies* 13 (Spring 1973): 166-74; Ellis, *Kellogg,* p. 11; Fox, *Clark,* pp. 503-30.

43. RDS1930, p. 6.

44. *New York Times,* Jan. 11, 1930, p. 3.

45. Ibid., Nov. 9, 1928, sec. 9, p. 1.

46. Fox, *Clark,* pp. 531-36.

47. *New York Times,* Jan. 11, 1930, p. 3; Feb. 6, 1930, p. 3. Clark's task took an ugly turn when a would-be assassin shot and nearly killed the new Mexican president after his oath of office.

48. Ibid., March 27, 1930, p. 29.

49. RDS1931, p. 52; see also Fox, *Clark,* pp. 536-43.

50. Smoot to Stimson, telegram, Oct. 14, 1930, file 123 Clark, J. Reuben Jr./21, RG59. For an analysis of Clark's attitudes toward United States–Mexican relations, see Martin B. Hickman, "The Ambassadorial Years: Some Insight," *BYU Studies* 13 (Spring 1973): 175-84.

51. *New York Times,* Oct. 4, 1930, p. 5; see also file 123 Clark, J. Reuben Jr./18, RG59.

52. *New York Times,* Oct. 4, 1930, p. 5.

53. Cline, *United States and Mexico,* pp. 210-12.

54. *New York Times,* Oct. 6, 1930, p. 22.

55. Ibid., Oct. 12, 1930, p. 2.

56. U.S., Department of State, *Press Releases,* Nov. 29, 1930, p. 1.

57. Fox, *Clark,* pp. 531-84.

58. Wilford Hardy Calcott, *The Western Hemisphere* (Austin: University of Texas Press, 1968), p. 254. See also James R. Garfield Diary, Manuscript Division, Library of Congress; Arthur Bliss Lane Papers, Sterling Memorial Library, Yale University, New Haven. Both of these embassy personnel had great respect for Morrow and Clark. See Lane to Stimson, telegram, Feb. 14, 1933, 123 Clark, J. Reuben Jr./83, RG59. Lane served as chief counsel at the embassy during the Clark tenure. He later (1944) became ambassador to Poland after serving similarly in several other countries.

59. Graham H. Stuart, *Latin America and the United States,* 5th ed. (New York: Appleton-Century Crofts, 1955), p. 173.

60. E. David Cronon, *Josephus Daniels in Mexico* (Madison: University of Wisconsin Press, 1960), pp. 12-13.

61. *New York Times,* Nov. 29, 1930, p. 8.

62. Cronon, *Daniels,* p. 77; see also Fox, *Clark,* pp. 544-84.

63. Smith, *Church History,* p. 645; Quinn, *Clark,* pp. 35-44.

64. ARC1933, p. 103.

65. S-ARC1933, p. 13.

66. Ibid., p. 103.

CHAPTER 6: PUTTING ON THE MANTLE

1. Feis to Herbert Cook, Jan. 27, 1934, 800.51/925; see also 800.51/1070, 1078, RG59.

2. R. Walton Moore to Stevens, Jan. 20, 1934, 839.51/4042, RG59; Diplomatic Serial 2386, 800.51/910A, RG59.

3. Hull (in Santiago, Chile) to Department of State, telegram, Jan. 5, 1934, 800.51/910, RG59. The council, nevertheless, stuck to its plans to work only with bonds in which the debtor government was involved. See SEC5, p. 78.

4. Jay to Baker, Jan. 11, 1934, Box 98, Baker MS. Baker's collection of correspondence with the council is particularly valuable because he seldom attended meetings and was largely a figurehead member. Hence, he received a large amount of memos, reports, and summaries to keep him informed about the activities of the council. Surprisingly, much of this material is not extant in the FBPC archives in New York.

5. See list of members as of December, 1934, FBPCAR1934, pp. 227-31.

6. Jay to Baker, Jan. 11, 1934, Box 98, Baker MS. Dulles had long been involved in the foreign bond problem and had helped in the establishment of the council.

7. Jay to L. B. Williams, copy, Jan. 27, 1934, Box 98, Baker MS.

8. Jay to Baker, Feb. 14, 1934, Box 98, Baker MS.

9. "The Committee regards the Secretaryship as second in importance only to the Presidency." FBPCAR1934, p. 19; Minutes of the Executive Committee, Feb. 26, 1934, FBPC45.

10. See Bell's official report, FBPCAR1934, pp. 68-76; the text of the final agreement (January) with Germany, ibid., pp. 77-78; both in Box 98, Baker MS.

11. See draft of S682 in JRCP417. The bill became law on April 12, 1934.

12. Jay to Baker, March 5, 1934, Box 98, Baker MS; Robert L. O'Brien (U.S. Tariff Commission) to Francis B. Sayre (assistant secretary of state),

Feb. 2, 1934, 800.51/920, RG59; William H. Wynne, "Foreign Bondholders Protective Organizations," *Yale Law Journal* 43 (1933); Max Winkler, "Protecting America's Stake Abroad," *Wharton Review of Finance and Commerce,* Feb. 1935, pp. 5-6, 15-16; Winkler to Hull, March, 1934, 800.51/979, RG59; Hull to Winkler, April 19, 1934, 800.51/979, RG59.

13. *Deseret News* (Salt Lake City), March 7, 12, 1934; *Salt Lake Tribune,* Feb. 24, 1934, March 8, 1934; *Salt Lake Telegram,* March 7, 1934; JHLDS, Feb. 23-March 12, 1934; Quinn, *Clark,* pp. 53-63.

14. *New York Times,* April 15, 1934, p. 31; Ronald, "National Organizations," p. 451.

15. SEC5, p. 194.

16. Clark's sermon at the conference concerned the nature of truth. "The first truth to which I wish to refer is the truth that truth is true." ACR1934, p. 92.

17. *Salt Lake Tribune,* April 4, 1934; JHLDS, April 3, 1934, p. 6.

18. JHLDS, April 3, 1934, p. 6.

19. Feis, *1933,* p. 267.

20. See the decree of Batista's puppet, Carlos Mendieta y Montefur, FBPCAR1934, pp. 49-52.

21. FBPCAR1934, p. 44. The commission indeed decided (June 18, 1934) that the Machado regime was not a de jure government and could not make contracts binding upon the republic. The council, of course, affirmed "that the conclusions of the commission have no foundation either in law, equity, or morals." The loans affected amounted to nearly $100 million.

22. Rublee to Feis, April 17, 1934, 800.51/980, RG59.

23. "There developed a series of informal conferences covering the possibilities of working out some permanent adjustment of Uruguay's foreign dollar debt situation." The council was extremely reluctant to discuss "in these times of depression any permanent adjustment," and by the end of 1934, the Uruguayan situation remained unsettled. FBPCAR1934, p. 99.

24. Throop to Baker, telegram, April 27, 1934; Baker to Throop, telegram, April 28, 1934, Box 98, Baker MS.

25. *New York Times,* May 3, 1934, p. 32; FBPCAR, pp. 25-26.

26. Clark, "Permanent Court," p. 1.

27. J. Reuben Clark, Jr., "Some Factors in the Proposed Post-War International Pattern," typescript, speech to the Los Angeles Bar Association, Feb. 24, 1944, JRCP228.

28. Memorandum to the file, Aug. 25, 1937, JRCP417.

29. J. Reuben Clark, Jr., "Systems of Pacific Settlement of International Disputes: A Program," *Unity,* Oct. 4, 1923, p. 42. This was part of Clark's own plan for international organization. He proposed a "World Congress" to codify international law and to outlaw war.

30. *New York Times*, May 17, 1934, pp. 1, 17. Richard W. Leopold, *The Growth of American Foreign Policy: A History* (New York: Alfred A. Knopf, 1962), p. 504, believed that "the Court plan might have won if it had not been for an overweening confidence inside the administration and an over-whelming pressure outside Congress." Its defeat in the Senate on January 29, 1935, marked a high point in the "resurgence of isolationism." Ibid., ch. 39.

31. FBPCAR1934, pp. 79-82.

32. Clark to Baker, May 29, 1934; "Statement of the Council on the May 29, 1934 Conclusion of the Berlin Conference," Box 98, Baker MS; see FBPCAR1934, pp. 82-85, for the text of the council statement.

33. FBPCAR1934, p. 85.

34. JHLDS, June 2, 1934, pp. 4, 13, 14.

35. *Salt Lake Tribune*, June 3, 1934, p. 1.

36. *Salt Lake Telegram*, June 2, 1934, p. 1.

37. Ibid.; *Deseret News* (Salt Lake City), June 2, 1934, p. 1; June 12, 1934, p. 1.

38. *Salt Lake Telegram*, June 19, 1934, p. 1; *New York Times*, June 19, 1934, p. 21.

39. *Deseret News*, June 12, 1934, p. 1; Quinn, *Clark*, pp. 62-67; Fox, *Clark*, p. 597.

40. Clark believed that criticism only strengthened a cause. See Clark, "They of the Last Wagon," *Improvement Era*, Nov. 1947, p. 747.

41. FBPCAR1934, p. 85.

42. Ibid., pp. 85-86; see also "Report of Pierre Jay, Laird Bell, and William Cumberland on the German Debt Conference of April-May, 1934," Box 98, Baker MS.

43. FBPCAR1934, p. 44; *Bulletin of the Institute of International Finance* 71 (July 17, 1934).

44. FBPCAR1934, p. 52.

45. Ibid., p. 95.

46. Feis to Clark, June 11, 1934, 800.51/1065A, RG59. Feis forwarded Wright's letter to the council offices.

47. Memorandum of conversation between Clark and Undersecretary of State William Phillips, June 28, 1934, 800.51/1074 1/2, RG59.

48. Leopold, *Foreign Policy*, p. 472.

49. Clark to Feis, June 20, 1934, 800.51/1059 1/2, RG59.

50. Feis to Clark, June 26, 1934, 800.51/1059 1/2, RG59.

51. The three were John Van A. MacMurray, William Dawson, and Arthur Bliss Lane, all from Clark's service in the department. Memorandum of conversation between Clark and Phillips, June 28, 1934, 800.51/1074 1/2, RG59. Indeed, the position remained open until 1938 when Clark himself filled it. FBPCAR1938, p. 1.

52. Sayre to Bernard Greensfelder, July 10, 1934, 800.51/1069, RG59. Greensfelder, a St. Louis lawyer, was campaigning for a plan by which the government would buy up the defaulted bonds and then negotiate for their services on the intergovernmental level.

53. FBPCAR1934, pp. 86-87.

54. Ibid., pp. 87, 90.

55. Ibid., p. 90; *New York Times,* July 14, 1934, p. 1; "Report of Executive Committee Action, Feb. 6, 1934 to July 17, 1934," Box 98, Baker MS.

56. Clark to Baker, July 25, 1934, Box 98, Baker MS. Baker replied with compliments for Clark's "great wisdom" in operation of the council, July 30, 1934, Box 98, Baker MS. See also FBPCAR1934, p. 26; *New York Times,* July 26, 1934, p. 31.

57. Minutes of the Meeting of the Board of Directors, July 25, 1934, FBPC45.

58. FBPCAR1934, p. 62.

59. Ibid.

60. Ibid.

61. *New York Times,* Aug. 17, 1934, pp. 1, 8; FBPCAR1934, pp. 62-67.

62. FBPCAR1934, p. 67; "Documents Relating to the Proposal of the Dominican Republic in Respect of its Dollar Bond Issues," Box 98, Baker MS.

63. Ronald, "National Organizations," p. 452.

64. Interview with Alice Popp (FBPC secretary), Brooklyn, New York, Aug. 27, 1985 (hereinafter Popp interview).

65. FBPCAR1934, p. 56a (Chile), 94 (Colombia), 98 (Peru). The emboldening power of the Dominican success was apparent in Clark's communications of August 22.

66. *Deseret News* (Salt Lake City), Aug. 27, 1934, p. 1.

67. J. Reuben Clark, Jr., "Salvaging American-Owned Foreign Bonds," unpublished manuscript, Sept. 1934, JRCP212. Much of the material in this article appeared subsequently in other Clark publications on the bond situation. See, for example, Clark, "Collecting on Defaulted Foreign Dollar Bonds," *American Journal of International Law* 34 (Jan. 1940).

68. See correspondence between Clark and *CHM* editors in JRCP212.

69. *Wall Street Journal,* Sept. 25, 1934, p. 3.

70. S-ACR1934, p. 1.

71. Ibid., pp. 97-98.

72. Ibid., p. 98. Clark was more concerned at this point about the ideas of such as Huey Long and Father Coughlin than of the New Deal, although he later believed that Roosevelt was dangerous to private property à la the income tax, which he saw as an ill-disguised attempt to redistribute wealth.

See Quinn, *Clark,* pp. 68-70.

73. Cronon, *Daniels,* p. 155.

74. Ibid., pp. 155-58; Fox, *Clark,* pp. 597-98.

75. Jay to Baker, Nov. 8, 1934, Box 98, Baker MS.

76. Feis, *1933,* p. 277. He believed that the council never adequately acknowledged his efforts.

77. Feis to Hull, Nov. 13, 1934, 800.51/1087, RG59; Memorandum to Directors, Nov. 15, 1934, Box 98, Baker MS.

78. FBPCAR1934, p. 26; *New York Times,* Dec. 13, 1934, p. 35. Stevens had resigned as a director in October, although Clark had wanted him to keep the title as an honor. Minutes of the Executive Committee, Oct. 23, 1934, FBPC45.

79. Minutes of the Executive Committee, Nov. 9 and Dec. 11, 1934, FBPC45.

80. SEC5, pp. 30-31. Lindert and Morton, "How Sovereign Debt Has Worked," pp. 231-32, present evidence to suggest that the nonrepayers of the 1930s suffered no punishments at all during postwar lending waves, that creditor nations paid no attention whatsoever to borrowers' credit histories, and that "the same interest premia were charged to those . . . that had repaid faithfully and those who had not."

81. J. Reuben Clark, Jr., "Enforcement of Service of Foreign Securities," typescript, speech to New Orleans Association of Commerce, Nov. 15, 1934, JRCP212. Pulling ideas from his days as a dollar diplomat, Clark called for "building up foreign trade [by sending] men abroad who can live abroad, work abroad and be contented, and they must be men who are good enough to become partners in the home concern." Three days before, he delivered essentially the same message to the convention of the National Association of Securities Commissioners in New Orleans, JRCP413.

82. J. Reuben Clark, Jr., "Foreign Securities," handwritten notes for speech at Federal Reserve Bank, New York City, Dec. 17, 1934, JRCP212.

83. *Robert Morris Associates Bulletin* (Sept. 1934).

84. J. Reuben Clark, Jr., "Foreign Securities in Default," typescript, speech at 23d Annual Convention of Investment Bankers Association of America, White Sulphur Springs, W. Va., Oct. 20, 1934, JRCP212.

85. See, for example, Department of State memorandum, April 26, 1934, 800.51/947, RG59. The cooperation of the department was particularly evident during the German negotiations of 1934. Roosevelt and department officials sent several diplomatic notes to Germany demanding equality of treatment for all foreign bondholders. Ronald, "National Organizations," pp. 452-53.

86. *New York Times,* Jan. 7, 1934, p. 31.

87. SEC5, pp. 177-81, 185.

88. Ibid., pp. 185-87; FBPCAR1934, pp. 53-56.

89. The members of the Cuban committee, formally organized at 90 Broad Street on Nov. 8, were George L. Burnham, Donald J. Cowling, F. W. Leamy, Bruce R. Payne, and John J. Rowe—all representatives of institutional holders—insurance companies and colleges. Clark purposely eliminated individual holders from consideration because it was too difficult to be certain of their motives. FBPCAR1934, p. 54; SEC5, pp. 205, 208-9.

90. SEC5, pp. 191-94.

91. Memorandum to the Directors of the FBPC, Inc., Nov. 15, 1934, JRCP412.

CHAPTER 7: A NOISE AND A SHAKING

1. ACR1935, p. 95.

2. Lindert and Morton, "How Sovereign Debt Has Worked," p. 233.

3. Jeffrey D. Sachs, "Introduction," in *Developing Country Debt,* ed. Sachs, pp. 22-23.

4. J. Reuben Clark, Jr., "Bond Club Speech," typescript, speech to Bond Club of New York, Jan. 16, 1935, JRCP212.

5. Ibid. Clark's specific task in this speech was to counter growing claims that the United States could hardly press its bond claims as long as it continued to refuse to accept responsibility for defaulted state and Confederacy bonds, mostly in British hands. His argument hinged upon British–American arbitrations, but excuses such as the Cubans were asserting (that an illegal regime had negotiated the issues) continued to muddle the council position.

6. Sachs, "Introduction," p. 1. See also Corm, "Indebtedness," pp. 67-79, for an indicting summary of the spiraling ill-effects of external indebtedness, especially when confronted with an international economic downturn.

7. *New York Times,* Jan. 17, 1935, p. 33; *New York Herald Tribune,* Jan. 17, 1935, p. 29.

8. Minutes of the Executive Committee, Dec. 11, 1934, FBPC45.

9. Draft of HR 2043, 800.51/1089, RG59.

10. Clark to Hull, Jan. 19, 1935, 800.51/1090, RG59; Leopold, *Foreign Policy,* pp. 500, 570.

11. Hull's comments on HR 2043, Jan. 30, 1935, 800.51/1089, RG59.

12. Memorandum of telephone conversation between Phillips and Rublee, Feb. 19, 1935, 800.51/1094, RG59.

13. See, for example, department memorandum on Winkler criticism of FBPC, April 2, 1935, 800.51/1103 1/4, RG59.

14. J. Reuben Clark, Jr., "Some Contentions of Defaulting Debtors,"

handwritten notes, undated, JRCP413.

15. Ibid.

16. J. Reuben Clark, Jr., "Lincoln Day Address," handwritten notes, address to Rotary Club, Provo, Utah, Feb. 13, 1935, JRCP213.

17. FBPCAR1935, pp. 30-38.

18. See ibid., pp. 39-72, for the memoranda and the council's fourteen-point summary of positions.

19. JHLDS, April 3, 1935. On the Brazilian situation, see FBPCAR1935, pp. 26-30. The payments were nevertheless up to date by the end of 1935. Ronald, "National Organizations," p. 453.

20. *Deseret News* (Salt Lake City), April 4, 1935, p. 1.

21. *New York Times,* Sept. 6, 1935, p. 26.

22. Ibid., Nov. 2, 1935, p. 23.

23. ACR1935, p. 94.

24. Martin B. Hickman, "J. Reuben Clark, Jr.: The Constitution and the Great Fundamentals," *BYU Studies* 13 (Spring 1973): 25-40.

25. Phillips to Clark, telegram, April 13, 1935, 800.51/1100A, RG59; memorandum of telephone conversation between Feis and White, April 15, 1935, 800.51/1100A, RG59. This mode of criticism was as old as the council itself. See, for example, *New York Times,* April 29, 1934, sec. 2, p. 9. The problem sprang from the inability of the council to get anticipated support from the foundations. By 1935, the anti-business vogue of New Deal America had only heightened this criticism considerably. The council had assumed by association all of the malignancies of culpable Wall Street.

26. Phillips to Feis, April 15, 1935, 800.51/1102, RG59; Feis to Phillips, April 15, 1935, 800.51/1102, RG59.

27. FBPCAR1935, pp. 73-77; *New York Times,* April 26, 1935, p. 32.

28. FBPCAR1935, p. 77.

29. Also cumbersome at the time was the preparation of the council's first annual report, then in its final stages of publication. Indicative of the public mood over the council, the press notices of its release (for example, *New York Times,* May 6, 1935, pp. 18, 30) dealt largely with financing rather than the council's work of 1934. See, however, pro-council editorials, *Salt Lake Tribune,* May 11, 1935, p. 8; *New York Times,* May 12, 1935, sec. 3, p. 1.

30. Douglas to Phillips, May 4, 1935, 800.51/1109, RG59.

31. White to Carr, May 9, 1935, 800.51/1138, RG59.

32. Attached to ibid. In November, White asked the Department of Commerce for the same favor. Hull told the puzzled secretary of commerce that the State Department was absolutely unwilling to put the council on routine distribution, but gave it information it thought useful, and suggested he do the same. Hull to Roper, Nov. 23, 1935, 800.51/1198, RG59.

33. Hoover to Welles, May 22, 1935, 800.51/1122, RG59.

34. Welles to Hoover, May 29, 1935, 800.51/1122, RG59.

35. Clark greeted his Utah followers with an attack on government attempts to remake the nation and to destroy completely the rights of the states. *Deseret News* (Salt Lake City), June 7, 1935, p. 1; *Salt Lake Tribune,* June 8, 1935, p. 3; JHLDS, June 7, 1935, pp. 11, 12.

36. *Des Moines Tribune,* June 4, 1935, p. 3.

37. *New York Times,* June 8, 1935, p. 25. White spoke at White Sulphur Springs, West Virginia, before the state's bankers' association. Of the nearly $6 billion of foreign bonds outstanding, said White, some one-third were in default and another $200 million in sinking funds, and interest payments were past due as of that date.

38. The council, on June 26, 1935, formed two bondholders' committees to negotiate on two Chilean issues. After the pattern of the Cuban Public Works committee of 1934, all of the members were representatives of institutional holders. FBPCAR1935, pp. 79-87.

39. The council announced on July 10, 1935, a settlement with Costa Rica for 50 percent interest and amortization for three years, then full service. *New York Times,* July 11, 1935, p. 40; FBPCAR1935, pp. 108-17. It subsequently developed, however, that the Costa Ricans could not reach even this service, and new negotiations became necessary. *New York Times,* Oct. 26, 1936, p. 30; FBPCAR1936, pp. 13, 299-309. For Czechoslovakia, see FBPCAR1936, p. 118; for Guatemala, pp. 120-22; and for Argentina, p. 13. See also Harold E. Peters, *The Foreign Debt of the Argentine Republic* (New York: AMS Press, 1934).

40. These were Bolivia, Colombia, Cuba, the Dominican Republic, El Salvador, Germany, Haiti, Hungary, Panama, Peru, Uruguay, and Yugoslavia. FBPCAR1935, pp. 26-130, passim. The council had nevertheless attempted to begin work with virtually all of the defaulters and most of the debtors whose payments were falling past due.

41. White was exercised over an editorial, "Multiple Protective Committees," *New York Journal of Commerce,* July 2, 1935, which attacked the council for its failure to standardize the procedure that was successful in Britain. White to Feis, July 10, 1935, 800.51/1135, RG59.

42. Feis to White, July 13, 1935, 800.51/ 1135, RG59.

43. See letters, 800.51/1138, RG59. Although Feis and White were friends, Feis expressed later his unhappiness with his former colleague's demeanor. Feis, *1933,* pp. 269, 276.

44. See, for example, Gene A. Sessions, ed., *Mormon Democrat: The Religious and Political Memoirs of James Henry Moyle,* 2d ed. (Salt Lake City: Signature Books, 1992), pp. 32-35, 340-41.

45. Clark to Salmon O. Levinson, Aug. 5, 1935, JRCP252.

46. J. Reuben Clark, Jr., "Notes for Testimony before SEC," handwritten

notes, Oct. 30, 1935, JRCP213.

47. Clark to Baker, Sept. 27, 1935, Box 98, Baker MS.

48. "Confidential Memorandum to the Directors of the Foreign Bond-holders Protective Council, Inc.," Oct. 1, 1935, Box 98, Baker MS.

49. S-ACR1935, p. 92.

50. Ibid.; Quinn, *Clark*, pp. 69-70.

51. Abe Fortas to E. C. Wilson, Oct. 15, 1935, 800.51/1191, RG59; Douglas to Hull, Oct. 28, 1935, 800.51/1190, RG59.

52. SEC5, pp. 1-3; *New York Times,* Oct. 23, 1935, p. 29.

53. SEC5, p. iii; see also William O. Douglas, *Democracy and Finance* (Port Washington, N.Y.: Kennikat Press, 1969), pp. 200-203.

54. *New York Times,* Oct. 31, 1935, p. 27. See list of members, FBPCAR1935, pp. 503-535.

55. *New York Times,* Oct. 31, 1935, pp. 27, 36.

56. Ibid., p. 36.

57. Ibid., Nov. 2, 1935, p. 23; Nov. 3, 1935, sec. 3, p. 1; Nov. 8, 1935, pp. 35-37; Nov. 9, 1935, p. 21; also pertinent excerpts of his testimony in SEC5, pp. 32-34, 78-92, 115-209, sec. 4 and sec. 5, passim.

58. See particularly *New York Times,* Nov. 2, 1935, p. 23.

59. JHLDS, Nov. 27, 1935, p. 5.

60. *Deseret News* (Salt Lake City), Nov. 27, 1935, p. 3.

61. *New York Times,* Dec. 5, 1935, p. 37.

62. FBPCAR1935, pp. 13-25. See *New York Times,* May 18, 1936, p. 25, for the press announcement of the issuance of the 1935 report. See also "Confidential Memorandum to the Directors of the Foreign Bondholders Protective Council, Inc.," Oct. 1, 1935, Box 98, Baker MS.

63. *Salt Lake Tribune,* Dec. 7, 1935, p. 12. Clark failed to mention (or to notice) that the revenues of many of these underdeveloped states were so miniscule that even a small percentage was a large amount in the relative sense—the widow's mite concept.

64. Ibid.; JHLDS, Dec. 6, 1935, p. 4.

65. By that time, there could be little doubt that the Reichsbank, for example, "not only permitted but encouraged" German exporters to use the foreign currencies they were receiving in payment for their products to repatriate bonds, although German financial authorities staunchly maintained that they were not releasing foreign exchange for such purposes. Harris, *Germany's Foreign Indebtedness,* pp. 34-35.

66. *Deseret News* (Salt Lake City), Dec. 9, 1935, p. 10; JHLDS, Dec. 9, p. 3; FBPCAR1935, p. 12.

67. J. Reuben Clark, Jr., "Compulsory Clearance," typescript, speech to the Kiwanis Club, Salt Lake City, Utah, Feb. 21, 1936, JRCP213. In this address, Clark rejected calls for the United States to follow the lead of the

British in collecting foreign debts by means of "compulsory clearance" whereby "private funds may be confiscated and applied to pay on private funds owed by nationals of the debtor nation to debtors of the creditor nation."

68. Leonard J. Arrington, "Origins of the Mormon Welfare System," *BYU Studies* 10 (Fall 1970); Arrington and Bitton, *Mormon Experience*, pp. 272-78.

69. *New York Times*, March 31, 1936, p. 27.

70. Quinn, *Clark*, pp. 73-75.

71. *New York Times*, May 25, 1936, p. 20.

CHAPTER 8: PROPHESYING UPON THE BONES

1. *New York Times*, Jan. 1, 1936, p. 41.

2. See pertinent excerpts of SEC5, passim.

3. *New York Times*, April 29, 1936, p. 32.

4. Ibid., May 7, 1936, p. 33.

5. Ibid., Aug. 24, 1936, p. 23.

6. SEC5, pp. 165-66.

7. Clark to Grace S. Heron, Dec. 21, 1935, JRCP352. To the inevitable frustration of the bondholders, government agencies also refused to give any sort of advice. Memorandum of telephone conversation with Sumner Welles, Sept. 8, 1936, JRCP417.

8. Clark to Noah Rogers, Dec. 21, 1935, JRCP352.

9. Clark to Heron, Dec. 21, 1935, JRCP352.

10. FBPCAR1936, pp. 6-7.

11. Draft of proposed legislation, May 2, 1936, JRCP412.

12. FBPCAR1936, pp. 7-8.

13. Ibid., p. 8.

14. Ibid., pp. 8-9.

15. Ibid., pp. 9-10.

16. Ibid., p. 10.

17. Ibid., p. 11.

18. *Salt Lake Tribune*, Sept. 1, 1936, p. 6; JHLDS, Aug. 31, 1936, p. 3.

19. S-ACR1936, pp. 11-114. See also J. Reuben Clark, Jr., "Testimony of the Divine Origins of the Welfare Plan," address delivered at Brigham Young University, Provo, Utah, Aug. 3, 1951; *Deseret News* (Salt Lake City), Aug. 8, 1951, church section.

20. Quinn, *Clark*, pp. 73-77.

21. *New York Times*, Jan. 21, 1937, p. 12.

22. Ibid., Jan. 23, 1937, p. 29.

23. Ibid., Feb. 18, 1937, p. 34.

24. Ibid., Jan. 21, 1937, p.12.

25. Feis to Hull, Nov. 13, 1934, 800.51/1087, RG59.

26. Clark to Baker, Feb. 18, 1937, Box 99, Baker MS. See also FBPC brochure, Aug. 15, 1936, JRCP212, outlining negotiations on 245 issues worth some $2.3 billion and urging bankers, manufacturers and exporters associations, and individuals to join.

27. FBPCAR1937, pp. 21-22; *New York Times*, Feb. 24, 1937, p. 34. See Iliana Zloch-Christy, *Debt Problems of Eastern Europe* (Cambridge: Cambridge University Press, 1987) for an analysis of the current crisis in that region.

28. *New York Post*, Feb. 27, 1937, p. 21.

29. Baker to Clark, March 1, 1937, Box 99, Baker MS. Baker naturally demanded to know what was going on.

30. Clark to Baker, March 3, 1937, Box 99, Baker MS.

31. *New York Post*, March 5, 1937, p. 21.

32. FBPCAR1936, pp. 14, 499-511.

33. FBPCAR1934, p. 82.

34. *Deseret News* (Salt Lake City), March 12, 1937, p. 1; JHLDS, March 12, 1937, p. 5. At the April conference of the church, Clark delivered one of his most memorable addresses. Illuminating clearly his foreboding worldview, he worried about the possibility of war and charted the philosophical course of neutrality he hoped the nation would "have the wisdom to follow." ACR1937, pp. 22-27.

35. White to Feis, March 26, 1937, 800.51/1243 1/2, RG59. White probably hoped Feis knew of the SEC results and would give him a clue. He either did not, or would not.

36. SEC5, p. 736; FBPCAR1937, p. 14.

37. SEC5, pp. 736ff.

38. "Roosevelt backs the SEC, so the effect of the Council lies in the balance," *New York Times*, May 15, 1937, p. 25.

39. "Collecting Foreign Debts," *Business Week*, May 22, 1937, p. 44.

40. FBPCAR1937, pp. 10, 781-82.

41. Clark to Feis, June 3, 1937, 800.51/1250, RG59; Feis to Welles, memorandum of conversation between Feis and James Landis, June 1, 1937, 800.51/1251, RG59.

42. Feis to Welles, memorandum of conversation between Clark and Feis, June 1, 1937, 800.51/1252, RG59.

43. *New York Times*, June 29, 1937, p. 29. Rumor had it that Clark was there to see the Brazilian mission in Washington over that country's bond situation, but he did not. He also carried copies of the 1936 annual report the council issued that same day. Ibid., June 28, 1937, p. 29.

44. Memorandum to the file, June 29, 1937, JRCP417.

45. See Quinn, *Clark,* pp. 221-36, for a surprisingly frank discussion of Clark's not so surprising set of racial attitudes.

46. Clark to Baker, July 3, 1937, Box 99, Baker MS. The directors normally met in the spring. At first, the customary month was February, but later it became April. See Clark to Baker, Feb. 18, 1937, Box 99, Baker MS.

47. FBPCAR1937, pp. 13-14, 784-90.

48. Clark to Hull, July 13, 1937, 800.51/1257, RG59; FBPCAR1937, p. 8.

49. Landis to White, July 21, 1937, 800.51/1261. RG59. In April of 1938, the council called a special meeting at which it further amended the bylaws to remedy this final objection, the "almost" in the first set of reforms. Douglas to Feis, April 8, 1938, 800.51/1292, RG59; FBPCAR1937, pp. 14-15.

50. Landis to White, July 21, 1937, 800.51/1261, RG59. See also *New York Times,* July 22, 1937, p. 29.

51. White to Feis, July 21, 1937, 800.51/1263, RG59; Feis to White, July 30, 1937, 800.51/1263, RG59; White to Feis, Aug. 3, 1937, 800.51/1269, RG59.

52. Grant told a group of young British Mormons to better themselves always. "I think I have accomplished a great deal in self-improvement since my 60th birthday." *New York Times,* Aug. 2, 1937, p. 21.

53. FBPCAR1937, pp. 20, 22-23. While in Geneva, the anti-League activist made a rather startling proposal. Presaging such post-World War II institutions as the World Bank and the International Monetary Fund, he discussed the possibility of international machinery "to control and prevent States from making loans when they were already practically insolvent." Memorandum to the file, Aug. 25, 1937, JRCP417. See also J. Reuben Clark, Jr., "Some Notes on Functions and Responsibilities of Paying Agents and Issue Houses," report to the League of Nations Committee for the Study of International Loan Contracts, Nov. 4, 1937, JRCP417.

54. Feis remembered this period of the council's history as follows: "In time their able handling of default situations became rather standard procedure and the State Department was called on to intervene less and less often—and less and less critically. Thus, those who had helped to create the organization could have a sense of satisfaction. But my own feelings were soured by a notion that the desire to secure payment from German authorities on loans which American banks had made to them was causing the financial community and certain elements of the business community to be too conciliatory toward the Hitler regime. It is the one area in which, I think, private American financial interest swayed—if only in a minor measure—American policy during the decade of the thirties." Feis, *1933,* p. 277. For an

expansion of this thesis but with regard to Latin American policy, see Robert White Hodge, "Lining up Latin America: The United States Attempts to Bring About Hemispheric Solidarity, 1939-1941," Ph.D. diss., Michigan State University, 1968.

55. *New York Times,* Sept. 19, 1937, sec. 2, p. 1; ACR1937, pp. 25-26.

56. S-ACR1937, p. 106.

57. Ibid.

58. *Salt Lake Telegram,* Oct. 16, 1937, p. 8; JHLDS, Oct. 15, 1937, p. 4.

59. Memorandum of telephone conversation with Douglas, Dec. 14, 1937, JRCP417.

60. Feis, *1933,* p. 277.

61. *Deseret News* (Salt Lake City), Dec. 22, 1937, p. 3; Clark to Feis, Dec. 17, 1937, 800.51/1278, RG59; FBPCAR1937, p. 8.

62. FBPCAR1937, p. 6; *Deseret News* (Salt Lake City), Dec. 22, 1937, p. 3. Several other committees followed suit within the next year, especially after the release of the endorsing Board of Visitors report. FBPCAR1937, p. 6; FBPCAR1938, p. 21; *New York Times,* Sept. 17, 1938, p. 24.

63. FBPCAR1937, pp. 8-13; *New York Times,* Jan. 9, 1938, sec. 3, p. 1.

64. *Salt Lake Telegram,* Jan. 8, 1938, p. 1; JHLDS, Jan. 8, 1938, p. 13.

65. Memorandum of Feis, Jan. [?], 1938, 800.51/1265, RG59.

66. Notice of Winkler's "Bond Letter" attacking FBPC, department for acquiescence, Jan. [?], 1938, 800.51/1274, RG59; Hoover to State Department, Jan. 22, 1938, 800.51/1285, RG59.

67. FBPCAR1937, p. 17.

68. Ibid., p. 9.

69. Ibid., pp. 9-10, 16-17.

70. Ibid., p. 14. See copy of amended bylaws, July 13, 1937, JRCP412.

71. FBPCAR1937, p. 15.

72. *New York Times,* May 22, 1938, sec. 3, p. 5.

73. Clark to Board of Directors, April 25, 1938, JRCP412.

74. FBPCAR1938, p. 1; *New York Times,* June 6, 1938, p. 25; *Deseret News* (Salt Lake City), May 28, 1938, p. 10; JHLDS, May 28, 1938, p. 1. The reorganized panel of officers consisted of White, president; Clark, chair of the executive committee; Laird Bell, vice president; and Dana G. Munro, vice president. Other members of the executive committee were Hendon Chubb, James Grafton Rogers, Thomas Thacher, and John C. Traphagen.

CHAPTER 9: PROPHESYING UNTO THE WIND

1. FBPCAR1938, pp. 16-20.

2. That summer, Clark recapitulated his four and a half years on the

Council in an article, "Foreign Bondholding in the United States," *American Journal of International Law* 32 (July 1938): 439-46.

3. S-ACR1938, p. 136.

4. Ibid.

5. Ibid.

6. *New York Times,* Nov. 17, 1938, p. 37. See Quinn, *Clark,* pp. 78-89, for a good summary of Clark's anti-Roosevelt sympathies and activities.

7. *New York Times,* June 21, 1939, p. 23.

8. Ibid., Dec. 16, 1939, p. 10.

9. In his figurehead position on the council, Clark did, however, remain close to the council's efforts. His work in the field became increasingly indirect and detached. See, for example, his "Collecting on Defaulted Foreign Dollar Bonds," *American Journal of International Law* 34 (Jan. 1940): 119-25.

10. *New York Times,* Nov. 21, 1945, p. 31. See also J. Reuben Clark, Jr., *Public Loans to Foreign Countries* (Salt Lake City: Deseret News Press, 1945).

11. J. Reuben Clark, Jr., "The North Atlantic Treaty, an Entangling Alliance," *Stand Fast by Our Constitution* (Salt Lake City: Deseret Book Company, 1962), pp. 85ff.

12. J. Reuben Clark, Jr., "Our Dwindling Sovereignty," address delivered at Salt Lake City, Feb. 13, 1952, JRCP245-46.

13. Among Clark's more typical speeches and writings touching upon the subject are "Slipping from Our Old Moorings," address delivered at Salt Lake City, March 5, 1947, JRCP236; *Some Political Blessings* (Salt Lake City: Bookcraft, 1957); *Stand Fast by Our Constitution;* "Dangers of Communism," address delivered at Salt Lake City, Oct. 6, 1959, JRCP249; "American Free Enterprise," address delivered at Salt Lake City, Dec. 6, 1946, JRCP235; "Inroads upon the Constitution by Roman Law," address delivered at Salt Lake City, Sept. 17, 1946, JRCP234; and "Let Us Have Peace," address delivered at Chicago, Nov. 14, 1943, JRCP237. For excellent if somewhat apologetic analyses of Clark's postwar thinking, see Martin B. Hickman and Ray C. Hillam, "J. Reuben Clark, Jr.: Political Isolationism Revisited," *Dialogue: A Journal of Mormon Thought* 7 (Spring 1972): 37-46; and James B. Allen, "J. Reuben Clark, Jr., on American Sovereignty and International Organization," *BYU Studies* 13 (Spring 1973): 185-95.

14. See Quinn, *Clark,* pp. 89ff., for the rest of Clark's career as Mormon leader.

15. Clark's obituary appeared in the *New York Times,* Oct. 7, 1961, p. 23.

16. FBPCAR1938, pp. 21-22.

17. *New York Times,* June 18, 1938, p. 7.

18. File 800.51/1300ff, RG59. Treasury finally denied the request on Dec. 2, 1938.

19. Welles to Feis, Aug. 12, 1938, 821.51/2221, RG59, summarized in 800.51/1315, RG59.

20. *New York Times,* June 18, 1938, sec. 3, p. 1; July 1, 1938, p. 23.

21. Ibid., July 7, 1939, p. 25; State Department to White, Aug. 11, 1939, 821.51/2374A, RG59.

22. David Green, *The Containment of Latin America: A History of the Myths and Realities of the Good Neighbor Policy* (Chicago: Quadrangle Books, 1971).

23. *New York Times,* Oct. 28, 1939, p. 1.

24. Littell Rust (Madison, Tenn.) to Roosevelt, Oct. 31, 1939, 800.51/1368, RG59.

25. *New York Times,* Oct. 31, 1939, p. 7. The two evidently appeared together before reporters.

26. FBPCAR1945, p. 7.

27. FBPCAR1945, pp. 4, 124. Contributions from bondholders on settlements became mandatory in 1943. "As part of the definitive offers, the contributions were deducted by the Paying Agents and transmitted to the Council. They were at the rate of $1.25 per $1,000 bond from 1935 to 1956; at the rate of $2.50 per $1,000 bond from 1957 until 1975; and from $5.00 to $7.50 per $1,000 bond from 1975 to 1979 (the year in which the last offer was made), and were deducted from the first interest payment only under a new readjustment plan or settlement offer." FBPC information, May 17, 1984, from Alice Popp.

28. FBPC, *Report, 1962-1964* (New York: The Council, 1965), p. v. Dana G. Munro of Princeton University was president at the time of this report. See his "Sweetening Sour Bond Issues," *World Affairs* 122 (Fall 1959): 81-96.

29. FBPC, *Report, 1962-1964,* pp. v-viii; Dragoslav Abramovic, *Debt Servicing Capacity and Postwar Growth in International Indebtedness* (Baltimore: Johns Hopkins University Press, 1958).

30. Morris Miller, *Coping Is Not Enough: The International Debt Crisis and the Roles of the World Bank and the International Monetary Fund* (New York: Dow Jones Irwin, 1986); Alexis Rieffel, *The Role of the Paris Club in Managing Debt Problems,* Essays in International Finance, no. 161 (Princeton, N.J.: Princeton University Department of Economics, 1985). In an analogy Clark would greatly appreciate, Rieffel (p. 2) likens the work of the IMF, the Paris Club, and the London Club to that of a three-ring circus. For a solid general analysis of the cause and immediate effects of the current crisis, see William R. Cline, *International Debt and the Stability of the World Economy* (Cambridge, Mass.: MIT Press, 1983).

31. Wylie had become a de facto officer of the council, and Rogers "did not want a female executive." Popp interview. Wylie in New York and VaLois South, Clark's secretary in Salt Lake City, had to become his alter egos while he sojourned during the thirties in the opposite city. See numerous memoranda and letters of the two in JRCP, particularly Box 416.

32. Popp interview. She received no compensation after 1975.

33. FBPC information, May 17, 1984, from Alice Popp.

EPILOGUE

1. World Bank figures, cited in Jim MacNeill, "Strategies for Sustainable Economic Development," *Scientific American,* September, 1989, pp. 155-65. MacNeill's article joined a rising chorus of opinion calling for the retiring of LDC debts as a crucial part of a plan to achieve sustainable development in the nineties, along with reforestation, soil conservation, slowing population growth, and developing renewable resources.

2. For a particularly good and concise dissection, see Barry Eichengreen and Richard Portes, "The Anatomy of Financial Crises," in *Threats to International Financial Stability,* ed. Richard Portes and Alexander Swoboda (Cambridge: Cambridge University Press, 1987), pp. 10-58.

3. Tony Killick, *Policy Economics: A Textbook of Applied Economics on Developing Countries* (London: Heinemann, 1981), p. 190.

4. Richard M. Alston and Timothy Tregarthen, *Economics* (New York: Worth Publishers, 1992), p. 41:40

5. Darrell Delamaide, *Debt Shock: The Full Story of the World Debt Crisis* (Garden City, N.Y.: Doubleday, 1984), p. 6. Delamaide presents a very readable, step-by-step analysis of the evolution of the current crisis.

6. Evans, *Dependent Development,* p. 79. Evans presented data indicating that U.S. direct investment as a proportion of total U.S. long-term investment in Latin America declined from 100 percent in 1897 to 68 percent in 1929, rose in the 1950s to 90 percent, and then went into steep decline again in the 1970s.

7. Killick, *Policy Economics,* pp. 189, 199-200.

8. Michael P. Dooley and C. Maxwell Watson, "Reinvigorating the Debt Strategy," *Finance & Development* 26 (Sept. 1989): 8. See also Jeffrey D. Sachs, *New Approaches to the Latin American Debt Crisis,* Essays in International Finance, no. 174 (Princeton, N.J.: Princeton University Department of Economics, 1989). A particularly lucid analysis of future possibilities from the LDC perspective is Miguel S. Wioncsek, "Where Do We Go From Here?" in *External Debt Crisis,* ed. Wionczek and Tomassini, pp. 437-59.

9. Stanley Fischer and Ishrat Husain, "Managing the Debt Crisis in the

1990s," *Finance and Development* 27 (June 1990): 24-27. See also "Resolving the International Debt Crisis," in *Developing Country Debt,* ed. Sachs, pp. 313-23.

10. Ibid., p. 25.

11. Ibid., p. 27. For a view of the current crisis from the right, and one more in keeping with the way Clark saw things in the 1930s, see Roger E. Shields, *Aspects of Current Debt Problems: Is the Problem Insolvency or Liquidity* (Washington: D.C.: American Enterprise Institute for Public Policy Research, 1985).

12. U.S., Central Intelligence Agency, figures, released to the press, December 5, 1990.

Index

A Note on the Author

GENE A. SESSIONS is John S. Hinckley Fellow and professor of history at Weber State University. He is the author of several previous histories, including *Mormon Thunder: A Documentary History of Jedediah Morgan Grant*, *Mormon Democrat: The Religious and Political Memoirs of James Henry Moyle*, and (with Donald R. Moorman) *Camp Floyd and the Mormons*.